DISCIPLESHIP & SPIRITUAL WARFARE

Kingdom Principles for Living Victoriously

John 6:40 — *"And this is the will of Him who sent Me, that everyone who sees the Son and believes in Him may have everlasting life…"*

Book 4

Nancy Williams

Way of Life Publishing

Nancy Williams
Copyright © 2009 by Nancy Williams
Revised 2016, 2023

No part of this book may be reproduced or transmitted in any form or by any means, electronic or mechanical, including photocopying and recording, or by any information storage or retrieval system except as may be expressly permitted in writing by the author. Permission requests are to be addressed in writing at AWayofLifeMinistries.com. All scripture quotations, unless otherwise indicated, are from the New King James Version.

ISBN: **979-8-9875825-3-4**

PRINTED IN THE UNITED STATES OF AMERICA

To order additional copies of this resource,

Visit: AWayofLifeMinistries.com, Barnes and Noble & Amazon.com

E-book available

DEDICATION

To those who read this:

> This is dedicated to you, in the hopes that through this book you will find a deeper meaning in your walk with Christ. I hope a living Christianity will be yours. That you feel how much you are loved; that you see more clearly how the Bible applies to you; and that you will then embrace and incorporate these principles into your way of being and living.

I want to thank and acknowledge my loving husband, Jaycee, and daughter, Natalie, for lovingly and graciously supporting me as I took time away to complete this labor of love.

PREMISE FOR THIS WORK

Based on Romans 3:23, where God says that all have sinned and fall short of the glory of God, it is this book's premise that all of us require healing. We believe it is through sin, starting with Adam and Eve and passed down from generation to generation, that dysfunctional patterns began. It is sin that separates us from God, says Isaiah 59:2.

It is our goal to facilitate:

    1st — Looking at ourselves honestly

    2nd—Accepting God's grace, love and truth so that

    3rd —We can be set free from our sins

We propose to do this by using God's Word and following His way.

We believe the fruit of this will be:

- An intimate relationship with God the Father, God the Son and God the Holy Spirit

- The abundant life from God will be ours as we live and grow in this dynamic relationship

- Manifestation of the gifts of the Spirit in us which is for the profit of all and that God gives as He sees fit and when He sees fit (1 Corinthians 12:7-11). These gifts of the spirit include:

    a. Word of wisdom

    b. Word of knowledge

    c. Faith

d. Gift of healing

e. Working of miracles

f. Gift of prophecy

g. Discerning of spirits

h. Gift of tongues

i. Interpretation of tongues

HOW TO USE THESE CHAPTERS

Bringing sinful patterns to the surface and dealing with them according to God's principles will restore your path in life and repair the breach separating you from others and from God, as stated in Isaiah 58:12. Individuals who have gone through this book have found the Holy Spirit and stated that they were empowered and enabled to trust God and look honestly at their lives.

God calls you and all of us to live a principled life. As you incorporate His principles in this book, the Holy Spirit will naturally flow through you to others. This book will cover 3 of God's principles as well as a growth plan and emphasizes God's principles, as found in the Bible, as the only source of living victoriously. As God created the world and set up universal principles by which it operates, relational principles are found within this creation and the Bible. He and His principles are the source of life and as you incorporate them, your life will flow smoother with less turmoil and more success. Therefore, memorize some of the given scriptures and the Holy Spirit will bring them to your remembrance in your time of need. "God's Word will not return void" (Isaiah 55:11). You will be affected by memorizing His Word even if you do not feel that an impact is being made. In each chapter, answer the questions to the best of your ability and you will be amazed at what starts happening within you!

This work is divided into 4 books which can be completed separately or sequentially by yourself or within a group setting.

If going through A Way of Life in a group setting, the facilitator may decide to share a short weekly teaching which provides the biblical foundation for the principle/s being reviewed, such as confession or repentance. The main group could then be divided into groups with a group facilitator present to promote sharing what God is doing in each other's lives, what the chapter review has brought to light and any hindrance in depending on God. The main facilitator may bring the whole group back together at the end for sharing and prayer or each group could end their time with prayer.

Additional supportive subjects are found in the appendix at the back of each book in this series of 4.

> And now, let us continue with discovering and applying God's Kingdom Principles for Living Victoriously!

INTRODUCTION

Looking at being a disciple of God's kingdom principles and learning of and following the leading of the Holy Spirit is what this book will walk you through. With Book 4 you will learn about fasting, listening to the Holy Spirit and His still small voice, spiritual warfare and how to put on your spiritual armor, as well as sharing these principles with others. I am excited for you! Stay the course. It's not always easy but it's worth it.

You might be thinking, "I'm nothing and no one thinks of me as much, so why would God?" The answer is that You are created in the image of God and hence, are very valuable and precious in His sight and loved unconditionally. You are worthy because He says so and He wants a relationship with you. You also have a purpose that you were born to fulfill and as you draw close to God and His way, you will become aware of and can then learn to live out what was ordained for you from the beginning of time.

Therefore, let's start this book by looking at your identity as a child of the Most High God. ☻

The Westminster Catechism states, in question 1 with the answer:

- "Q. 1. What is the chief end of man?
- Man's chief end is to glorify God, and to enjoy him forever. 1 Cor. 10:31; Rom. 11:36; Ps. 73:25-28."

So, your goal is to get to know God and enjoy Him and as you do that (and in spite of), He enjoys you as well!

Before beginning, it's important to evaluate how you show up in life and look at how Jesus showed up, as He is our example to follow. You might be saying to yourself, "What is meant by how you show up?" In relationships with others, this means, are your moods and spirit happy, anxious, sad, overbearing, funny, serious, demanding, irritating, or goofy, to name a few. It's what you dole or give out to others and their experience of you. Jesus showed up with tough yet unconditional love for others and knew their heart motives and feelings. The way He showed up was compassionate and He listened well. Jesus could tell when some of the religious leaders were trying to trick Him and called them out about it. His heart was one for them to understand the will of His Father and for them to hear Him, but the religious rulers did not. Those that did, allowed Him to change them from the inside out as they got revelation or understanding about what love truly is and how God calls us to act, or *be, from the inside out.*

WHAT DOES IT MEAN TO BE?

You might have heard well-meaning messages about loving one another and treating each other with compassion and kindness while doing what's right. And yet, this message misses the mark. You might attempt to *put on* these character traits rather than *be* them on the inside and then wonder why the results are not evident. Loving, authentic Christianity is not the witness. So why is this? God created you to *be* love and when you are not, there's no authenticity nor behaving from the core of who you were created to be.

Here's your example:

1. Jesus was and is love
2. Jesus loved

Jesus came from an unconditional, divine state of being so He could then love in human flesh. Then and only then, could He manifest in power, effect and results. He chose to *be* love and is love. The difference is becoming love (a noun) on the inside instead of attempting to put it on and act loving on the outside when you aren't that on the inside. You may attempt to be what you are not which is what Jesus came to change. Transformation is the process and freedom is the result. Free to be who you were created to be!

So, like Jesus, you are to live and *be*, powered by the choice to love and be love. Being love is by choice, intention and commitment, empowered by His Holy Spirit. When you choose love and allow the Holy Spirit to guide you, you are your authentic self.

Remember, others live with you and maybe even more importantly, you live with yourself. The million-dollar question is, "How do you want to live with yourself?" Would you want to be the type of person who is open, calm, joyful, authentic, honest and loving, or the opposite? If you want the former, you get to choose to follow the example Jesus gave you of unconditional, authentic love. Then abundant life can flow through you to others and this life can be true, pure and lovely. When you are unconditional love, you are truly free.

> Free to fly to the music of His joy,
> Free to feel the waves tumble us in playfulness,
> Free Choice—
> The way it is meant to be.

THE HOLY SPIRIT

In this world, the war against good and evil is extremely evident. On one side is the good side, with peace and harmony. The other side is dark, which is evil. There is a call on the dark side to all who will hear to succumb to the pull of power, anger, death and destruction. This evil pull is so strong that it separates families, friends and even those in power.

God, in the person of the Holy Spirit, is a counselor and giver of knowledge and wisdom. God, in the person of the Holy Spirit, will come into your heart to be your guide and strength if you ask Him to! How this works will be covered throughout the rest of this book.

There are good and evil forces at work around you, ALL the time. You may or may not be aware of the evil temptations that pull you to do wrong things. To become a warrior of God, this work will support you in becoming more aware as well as increasing your connection with the Holy Spirit. You will learn how the Holy Spirit can guide you into all truth and warn you of danger, to list a few of the works He does!

As an example of how the Holy Spirit may talk to you, I will share an experience I had where the Holy Spirit gave me a gift of knowledge. At a church I was attending, I was on the prayer team. A lady wanted prayer and as I interviewed her, she told me why she needed prayer. While I prayed for what she wanted, the Holy Spirit as a still small voice inside of me kept impressing me to ask about her boyfriend. In obedience, I asked her about her boyfriend and she was SHOCKED! "How did you know?" she asked. I said that God revealed this to me so she could be set free because He loved her. That night, she was set free when we prayed for her real need.

God works to free His people and the workers are few. That is why this book was written. This book is for you, who are open to the light, want to live victoriously and tell others the good news!

CONTENTS

DEDICATION iii
PREMISE FOR THIS WORK iv
HOW TO USE THESE CHAPTERS vi
INTRODUCTION viii
CHAPTER 1 FASTING, HONESTY & SPIRITUAL WARFARE 1
CHAPTER 2 SILENCE AND SUBMISSION 22
CHAPTER 3 SHARING GOD'S KINGDOM PRINCIPLES WITH OTHERS 36
CHAPTER 4 SANCTIFICATION: PERSONAL GROWTH PLAN FOR ASSIMILATION & PRINCIPLE PRACTICE 44
CONCLUSION 49
SUGGESTED READING LIST 50
APPENDIX 53
USING A WAY OF LIFE IN GROUP SETTINGS 54
DEPENDENCE ON GOD 57
STRESS MANAGEMENT 59
THE SOCIAL READJUSTMENT RATING SCALE 67
TITHING 72
YEAR AT A GLANCE 76
YEAR AT A GLANCE – EXTRA BILLS 78
COMMUNICATION 80
GOAL SETTING 90
BIBLIOGRAPHY 96
ABOUT THE AUTHOR 101

As each part of A Way of Life can be purchased separately, some of the same writings are duplicated in some or each part of this book series. Examples include the growth plan and in the appendix, goal setting.

CHAPTER 1

FASTING, HONESTY & SPIRITUAL WARFARE

As you may have come through A Way of Life (books 1-3), you have seen how God desires for you to walk. Book 4 covers how to maintain this walk so that you do not go back to old ways. You may have come from, "I am a wretched human being" to "I am a child of the Living God! I am special, molded for His unique plan for me! I have a purpose! I am living in the present, not the past!" Romans 6:8 says, "Now if we died with Christ, we believe that we shall also live with Him." That is true not only for the future but also for now. "Likewise...reckon yourselves to be dead indeed to sin, but alive to God in Christ Jesus our Lord. Therefore, do not let sin reign in your mortal body, that you should obey it in its lusts...for sin shall not have dominion over you..." (Romans 6:12-14). The command is clear and you get to choose to believe it and walk in His way for you.

This chapter incorporates using all the previous principles of God covered in the first 3 books. Books 1-3 were designed to help you release your emotions and accept the freedom from guilt and sin's power over you that Jesus broke on the cross. These books also showed how much God loves you and that there is a plan for your life. Jesus gives all of this to you if you accept (for you) that He died on the cross and rose again that third day to pay the penalty of your sins—past, present and future.

Book 1 puts you in the right place to take an accurate, personal self-evaluation in Book 2. Books 2 and 3 include confession, repentance, reconciliation and forgiveness as well as an attitude of readiness and willingness to have what you see in yourself removed or refined. Now, let's move on to other helpful self-evaluation tools to support being honest quickly. This is so you can continue to walk in the cycle of confession, repentance, forgiveness and reconciliation which brings joy in being forgiven and free.

SPIRITUAL EVALUATION

J. Keith Miller, in A Hunger For Healing (N.Y.: Harper Collins, 1991), says that the three most common types of spiritual evaluations are the:

- On-the-spot check
- Daily examination
- Periodic examination

The spot check is immediate, which requires a conscious attitude of hearing the Holy Spirit as He checks you on something. The daily inventory is best started in the morning by asking God to show you during the day (on-the-spot checks) your erroneous ways and then reviewing them with Him in the evening, looking toward change. The point is not becoming obsessed with monitoring yourself but depending on God and the Holy Spirit to show what you are ready to see in yourself. God is in control over your healing and your sanctification process, "for it is God who works in you both to will and to do for His good pleasure" (Philippians 2:13). If you walk God's way, sanctification/healing ***will*** happen!

The daily examination speaks of living attentively while not being obsessive. It asks you to do preventive maintenance and diligence to bring all of you to God in prayer. Walking with God is keeping short accounts with Him, so that the freedom you have experienced may continue. Cultivating the godly habit of conversing with God throughout the day and taking to Him all the concerns and cares that you have will keep you in tune with Him. Your antennae will be up. Therefore, if you decide to incorporate doing a daily examination in your life, you will be following God's way. Watch how the Holy Spirit will begin to talk to and lead you. Daily take what the Holy Spirit shows you of your strengths, weaknesses, motives and behaviors. Lay them all before God and watch what happens! How do you do that?

In taking all your cares to Him, imagine tossing a basketball into a closed net and the basketball stays there, right? With God, toss Him your care, He catches it and keeps it. You *leave it* there in His hands (the closed net). Throughout your day, toss your concerns, worries, frustrations and triumphs into His hands and watch what happens to you on the inside.

An important element in your daily examination is not being a harsh judge of yourself, as you aren't loving yourself when you derate or think you "should be" a different way. Let yourself off the hook. The Holy Spirit will show you what you are to know about where your thoughts and emotions are coming from (i.e., motives, hurts) *IF* you *sincerely* ask Him to. God says, in John 16:13, "When He, the Spirit of truth has come, He will guide you into all truth...and He will tell you things to come." Therefore, you can depend upon the Holy Spirit for discernment (being able to tell the difference between lies and truth), as you will be bombarded by your flesh, the world, Satan (the father of lies—John 8:44) and his fellow demon liars. Satan and his forces seek to derail and condemn you, so be aware and don't let that happen. You won't be derailed if you stay honest with God and yourself while incorporating God's principles of honesty, confession, repentance, forgiveness and reconciliation into your life.

A helpful tool for any personal examination is writing in a journal. Writing can be a helpful way of keeping a daily inventory. It can be done as often and in any way you desire. You can begin a journal entry as a letter to God such as, Dear Lord, or however you want. You can write what is happening with you, what you feel God has been showing you, where you think He is leading you and thank Him for being there with you. As you do this, clarity or realizations may come about whatever you are writing about. This happened to me often as I journaled over the years. In looking at my old journals, I feel pleased and thankful to see the healing and growth God has wrought in me. So far have I come, yet so far do I have to go! I encourage you to make use of the written word to help clarify thoughts and emotions racing around within you by writing in a journal. The matchless benefit will be a clear mind and eventually, a clear direction!

The periodic examination can be done monthly or yearly. Take time for yourself to reflect on your growth. Read your journals and identify what is going on. You will know if you are on the right road or not and whether you get to repair a relationship that may have become tainted. God will bless your efforts!

A resource to use as part of any type of inventory is a book and website titled, How We Love (CO: Alive Communications, 2017) and HowWeLove.com, by Milan & Kay Yerkovich. In these resources, you will learn the type of parenting you grew up with and why your communication pattern is what it is. Learning your communication style can help point towards why your relationships are where they are at, today. My husband and I both used the avoider communication style which at first made it seem like we had a great relationship! As time went on, we learned that we were just avoiding what we needed to talk about and thankfully, began talking. The good news is everything can be tweaked and improved upon. This workbook is not about covering this extensive subject, but I will list the main communication styles that are called out on the website, and you may see yourself in one of these:

- Pleaser
- Avoider
- Vacillator
- Controller
- Victim
- The Secure Connector

Scripture to memorize: John 16:13, "When He, the Spirit of truth, has come, He will guide you into all truth...and He will tell you things to come."

SPIRITUAL WARFARE

All warfare, in a sense, is from Satan because of the fall of mankind and can be divided into direct and indirect warfare. Direct warfare is with Satan and his demons while indirect warfare comes from within your flesh and through our society (the world with its lusts, power and lies). If Satan can affect you through the indirect method, then he can leave you alone to work out your own destruction. The world, in a direct or indirect way, will pull at your flesh and be ever before you, bombarding your senses every day. This is why it's imperative to know how to spiritually defend yourself.

FIGHTING THE FLESH

Romans 6 calls you to not let sin reign in your mortal body, for until you see Jesus, you still live in fallen human flesh that resists the redeemed spirit within. In Romans 7, Paul gives a personal illustration: "...in my inner being I delight in God's law; but I see another law at work in me, waging war against the law of my mind and making me a prisoner of the law of sin at work within me" (vv.22-25). All Christians, from the mature Apostle Paul to the newest believer, have experienced the temptation cycle described in James 1:14-15. This starts with a desire, which you can choose to dwell on but if you do, your emotions will become stirred up. With the emotions stirred up, your desire increases. If you continue to nurse and rehearse that desire, you will get to the point of no return and act on your desire, resulting in sin and its terrible consequences.

How do you manage your flesh? You first get to evaluate what is going on. Ask, "Am I tired and feeling a certain way due to lack of sleep or food? Are my closest relationships on open terms? Am I anxious about something? If a female, is it time for my monthly cycle? Is there a miscommunication with my spouse, family, or friend?"

If you cannot identify the reason for difficult emotions, feelings, or thoughts, do not despair! God commands us to cast away or cast "down arguments and every high thing that exalts itself against the knowledge of God, bringing every thought into captivity to the obedience of Christ" (2 Corinthians 10:5). What this means is to throw away any thoughts that show up in your mind, that are lies. Picture the Word of God written on the backboard of your mind. When the troublesome thought comes, scan the backboard and evaluate whether that thought conforms to God's Word and if not, it's likely a lie. Immediately toss it out of your mind.

Using anger as an example, the Lord says in Ephesians 4:26-27, "Be angry, and do not sin: Do not let the sun go down on your wrath, nor give place to the devil." What this means, is you are giving place to the devil if you don't communicate or repair a relationship that is sour before you go to bed and the anger will continue to fester. As you hold onto anger, bitterness builds itself a root in you, which becomes Satan's foothold to beat you down. Again, allowing a root of bitterness to be planted and grow by not addressing issues, is giving place to the devil. It is laying a foundation with the enemy's tool of anger and bitterness, not God's way of honesty, confession, repentance and reconciliation.

Therefore, it is important to deal immediately with anger and other potentially negative emotions by speaking honestly yet gently with friends, your family and God. Then, you get to let go of the emotions as talked about in Book 1. In Ephesians 4:26-27, God says to be angry but not to *react* with sinning behavior when you feel your anger. God gives you permission to be angry as it tells you that something is not right. Maybe someone is hurting you or hurting someone that you care about. Or maybe your anger is hurtful to others because you have been hurt in the past and have not yet resolved those feelings and hurts. Anger is a valuable emotion (if used correctly) and learning from it will tell you much about yourself and what is going on around you, so you can decide on a godly course of action.

FIGHTING THE WORLD

With the world, you must be careful in what you subject your eyes, mind and heart to. Satan has perverted God's creation and principles so much that you must be careful of the magazines, books, movies, television shows, soap operas (they teach something other than God's beautifully ordained way of relating), MTV, pornography and anything else that speaks lies and perversions of God's ways. There is no way you can prevent all from getting in, but you can control the amount you subject yourself to. You get to learn to detect the lies and unreality, as Satan's perversions are there. The best way to protect yourself is to know God and His ways by being a diligent student of His Word.

An example of this is how a bank teller is trained. To be able to feel the fake money, the bank teller handles the real money over and over and over until the teller can tell the difference between the fake and real bills. The bank teller doesn't study the fake money, but the real. This example speaks to studying God's true way and when you do, you will know the fake, perverted truth (lie) when it comes around.

FIGHTING THE DEVIL

Regarding Satan and his demons, Ephesians 6 explains that spiritual warfare is not ultimately against flesh and blood, but against principalities, powers, the rulers of the darkness of this age and against spiritual hosts of wickedness in the heavenly places (v.12). You may have a spear of fear going through your heart reading this but there is no cause for concern. God has provided the way to protect yourself.

Here is God's provision for you: "Take up the whole armor of God, that you may be able to withstand in the evil day [a promise] having girded your waist with truth, having put on the breastplate of righteousness, and having shod your feet with above all, the gospel of peace; taking the shield of faith with which you will be able to quench all the fiery darts of the wicked one. And take the helmet of salvation, and the sword of the Spirit, which is the Word of God, praying always with all prayer and supplication in the Spirit, being watchful to this end with all perseverance and supplication for all the saints" (vv. 13-18). You get to pray for yourself and others and put on the armor of God to fight the enemy who seeks to destroy you and your loved ones.

Waking up each morning and intentionally speaking God's armor over yourself is very powerful in walking God's way and preparing yourself for the daily battle between the evil way and God's way (holy, righteous and good). Satan and his minions want to create fear in you as well as kill and destroy you. Satan wants to prevent you from moving into God's path for you, so always be prepared!

To give you an example that Satan and/or his minions like to attack us where or when we are vulnerable, I'll share what happened to me in Arizona. I was taking a nap at an extended family home and was just drifting off when I felt the bed go down on my left. I felt something cross my body (all the while my eyes were closed) and the bed went down higher up on my right side. I felt as though I was paralyzed and couldn't move. Immediately, it was as if there was crazy screaming and hands twitching violently in front of my closed eyes. Knowing that God is Lord over all demons and that demons MUST desist and leave in His name, I said Jesus' name and immediately, the demon left. Knowing that I was safe, I drifted off to sleep.

This is just one example that you who *truly know Jesus and have accepted Him into your heart*, as talked about in Book 1, are protected in His name and can call on Him to protect you. Remember, Jesus won the battle between Satan and his minions when He rose from the dead. Additionally, when you accepted what Jesus did for you, that exceeding greatness of His power that rose Jesus from the dead is also directed towards you (Ephesians 1:19). There's even more to know but this book is not written to cover all. To learn more, I highly recommend reading Pigs in the Parlor (MO: Impact Books. 1973), The Person and Work of the Holy Spirit (MI: Zondervan Publishing, 1974) and True Spirituality (IL: Tyndale House, 1971), listed in the bibliography. Be blessed as you learn more and more of Him!

KINGS, PRIESTS AND SAINTS

Revelation 1:6 and 5:10 state that God has "made us kings and priests." That means you are clothed in royal dignity and called to royal dominion. First Peter 2:5 declares, "You...are being built up [as]...a holy priesthood, to offer up spiritual sacrifices." You are in a priestly fraternity and priests are mediators, who bring others to

God. A king is one who rules with authority and power. So, are you wallowing in defeat? Why? Rise up and fight, stepping out as the priest and king that you are!

Is there anything hindering you from accepting what God says you are--a priest and a king? Are you feeling unworthy? None of us are worthy, but God saw fit to send Jesus as your and our savior and mediator. He then calls you and us all sons, daughters, priests and kings because we are His. Not by anything you or we do but because He says so. So, accept WHO and WHOSE you are & that He made you to be a priest and king!

Revelation 5:8 speaks of "the prayers of the saints." If you have accepted Jesus' death and resurrection for your sins, you are called a saint! The Greek word, hagios, translated as "saints," means to be set apart, to share in God's purity, to be blameless, sacred and pure. Christians are holy through the atoning work of Jesus. God sees you without spot or blemish through what Jesus did on the cross for you. He sees you as flawless and set apart. As a Christian, do you see yourself as God sees you? If not, you will experience defeat. If so, you will experience victory!

Write down any other hindrances you feel in accepting the fact that as a child of God you are a priest, saint and king:

A Way Of Life

Now, take these hindrances to God and ask Him to remove them, confess your unbelief and choose to believe. Choosing to believe and speaking what God says is true about you is key to keeping the victory in Christ that you have, as His child. Does that mean that you will do things right all the time? Of course not, but the key is to confess it immediately and decide to turn from it (repentance).

Describe a situation where you were recently wrong and admitted it immediately:

What were your feelings before and after?

Cite an example that shows you are learning new ways of interacting with others:

What does God say about what you are to do when others wrong you? Are you to confront them? Jesus said, "If your brother sins against you, go and tell him about his fault between you and him alone. If he hears you, you have gained your brother" (Matthew 18:15). It does not say to go to Sally or Joe and gossip, but to the brother who wronged you.

Going to the person directly involved is God's way of solving problems within the church with other saints or outside of the church (use wisdom and restraint in confronting non-Christians). You may hesitate to go to the person because of fear but giving into fear only perpetuates the division in the relationship, and God's way is harmony and unity. The other person will likely, due to their human nature, continue the way they are unless you or someone else (ex., your boss) holds them accountable. Image a society where everyone holds themselves accountable! That would be heaven and God's way is just that; everyone to hold themselves accountable for their own wrongdoings.

Therefore, holding yourself and others accountable to the way God has outlined for you and them to act in the scriptures, fosters everyone's spiritual growth. Love is shown to others when you care enough to confront and talk through issues (see Communication and

Confrontation in the appendix). They may rebel and run, but that is their responsibility before God. Just make sure you are responsible before Him to do your part. An example of when I confronted who I thought was another saint (believer in Jesus) is the following:

> I was in the process of copyrighting the ministry titled A Way of Life and hired who I thought was a Christian lawyer. Money was paid and the forms were filled out correctly. After many months of follow-up (8 months) I received a letter advising me that my copyright was declined as someone else, 6 months earlier, had applied and obtained the same name.
>
> I became aware that my lawyer had not filed my copyright forms in a timely manner, so I lost my ministry name. I went to him, as a fellow Christian, and asked for a refund due to his negligence in submitting my paperwork right away. He refused. After multiple attempts as well as asking, on my part, for both of us to go to the elders of his church and him refusing, I finally realized this lawyer may not really be a Christian. He certainly wasn't following God's way (Matt. 18:15-18). So, I took him to small claims court and won.
>
> When I arrived at his office to collect my check, I noticed that his office had been cleaned out and organized impeccably. I got my money back but more importantly, this individual learned that he was accountable. He took steps to clean up his office so others would get the timely service that they paid for and hopefully, then wouldn't sue him. The lawyer and others benefited, and I later got my ministry name anyway!

The point of sharing the above is to say, it is important to address issues and to address them in a biblical way. Take time away to also think about what is happening and search the scriptures to glean wisdom. If in doubt, ask your pastor or mature, spirit-filled Christian friend.

Describe an example where you confronted your brother:

What did you learn from confronting another?

Describe an example where you did not confront but should have:

A Way Of Life

What feelings were not resolved?

What effect did that have on you?

How much time do you spend evaluating and reflecting on your life and actions?

How many minutes of silence do you allow in your life?

In Joyce Huggett's book, The Joy of Listening to God, there is an example of a jar filled with water and sand. When the jar is shaken, the water is cloudy. As the jar rests, the sand settles to the bottom and the water becomes clear. It is the same with your life. Sometimes, your life's pace can cloud your perceptions and listening skills. As you allow rest and silence, you can hear God speak and work within you, resulting in clear perceptions and direction in what steps to take in situations you find yourself in. The call is to stop, rest and enjoy some silence.

FASTING

Did you know that God expects you to fast as part of your spiritual walk? Jesus fasted. Jesus fasted and prayed for 40 days and 40 nights and was able to resist the devil's temptations. Yet, most Christians have never been taught about the biblical benefits of fasting and then don't understand why they feel powerless. The following will support the understanding of what Jesus expects of his followers and it will help you unclog your straw so that rivers of living water (God's Holy Spirit and way) will flow from you to a dying world.

Another way to listen to God is through the discipline of fasting. The following work, written by Pastor Bill Robison, is adapted and used with permission.

What is the first thought that comes to your mind when you think of fasting? Do you picture some Buddhist monk or Hindu devotee? Perhaps the idea of fasting in a high-tech world seems rather archaic. There might be some super-spiritual types who don't go to work and who have time for this sort of thing, but how about a busy 40 + hour-a-week type?

Fasting is probably the most misunderstood and least practiced blessing that God has given to us so that we might draw closer to Him. Perhaps one reason is that it is practiced in all religions. Another reason is that in an age of fat phobia, fasting for physical rather than spiritual reasons is rather commonplace! Did you know that fasting is biblical and has always been part of the practice of God's church throughout history?

During the time of Jesus, fasting was a common practice among the Jewish people. John the Baptist and Jesus Himself practiced fasting when seeking the will of God. Even though it became a legalistic practice when used by the Pharisees, these scriptures reveal the biblical basis for fasting: Leviticus 23:27-28, Isaiah 58:1-7, Daniel 10:1-12, Nehemiah 1:4-11 and Esther 4:13-17. Fasting was always a part of the nation of Israel's life. We know that Moses, David and Elijah fasted.

The early church practiced voluntary fasting rather than the mandatory form found in the Jewish tradition. By the second century, there were two days of voluntary fasting a week: Wednesday and Friday.

As the church became more institutionalized, fasting became more legalized and was misconstrued to be a form of penance useful in winning God's favor. After the time of martyrdom ceased, monks became the new heroes. The big thing was who could fast the longest. Unfortunately, it became more of a pseudo-spiritual ego trip rather than what God intended fasting to be.

When the Protestant Reformation came about, many churches who wanted to break all ties with Catholicism had little use for fasting. In a very reactionary way, they threw out the baby with the bath water! Five hundred years have passed, and fasting is still only minimally emphasized. How many sermons have you heard about it?

WHAT IS FASTING?

Here is a simple definition: Fasting is abstaining from drink, food or both to draw closer to God. In an age with so many things that draw our attention, food and drink are primary things which do just that. We also say that fasting is the voluntary denial of an otherwise normal function for the sake of intense spiritual activity. Fasting is a useful tool for seeking a deeper level of communion with God in prayer and meditation, receiving guidance in decision making and experiencing intimate fellowship with Him. An important issue to understand is that fasting is not done to appease or manipulate God.

PROBLEMS WITH FASTING

There are four basic problems with fasting today. First, fasting has a bad reputation. Second, most people are generally uninformed about it. Third, we have many misconceptions about our body's need for food. Finally, we have some misconceptions about the act of fasting itself.

Jesus Christ clearly taught on fasting and fasted Himself. In Luke 4:1-13, we see that He fasted for 40 days without food. It does not say He went without liquids.

Matthew 6:16-18 instructs, "When you fast, do not be like the hypocrites, with a sad countenance. For they disfigure their faces so that they may appear to men to be fasting. Assuredly, I say to you, they have their reward. But you, when you fast, anoint your head and wash your face, so that you do not appear to men to be fasting,

A Way Of Life

but to your Father who is in the secret place; and your Father who sees in secret will reward you openly." Notice that Jesus did not attack the act of fasting or the frequency of it. As a matter of fact, Jesus assumed His disciples would fast. Fasting is to be part of the life of a Christian. What Jesus did attack is fasting to impress people with one's supposed spirituality. As usual, Christ gets to the heart of the matter: He's concerned with WHY we fast, not just that we do it.

BASIC MODELS

There are three basic models of fasting in Scripture.

- We see a partial fast in Daniel 10:3. In this type of fast, a person goes without certain kinds of food or drink for a set time. Wisdom should be used when on a liquid fast rather than on a food fast because God designed the human body to require liquids much more often than food

- The type of fast we see in Acts 9:9 and in numerous Old Testament scriptures is the complete fast or abstinence from food and drink for a period of time

- Finally, we see the corporate fast, in which the whole nation was called to participate in Leviticus 23:27 and Joel 2:15

There may be other types of fasts to help you focus on meeting with God. What distracts you or preoccupies you? For some, perhaps a fast from television, radio, movies, videos or music would be appropriate. How about a fast from sports or fasting from sitting on the couch for long periods of time (like all evening)? Maybe fast by refraining from talking on the phone or just from talking! Find out personally how silence teaches one to listen well and speak more wisely.

HOW LONG SHOULD ONE FAST?

Remember the purpose of fasting. The issue is not how long the fast is, but whether you are meeting God. I have fasted for a long time and not met God; I have fasted for only a short time and experienced wonderful times with Him. Some people fast from 6 p.m. until 6 p.m. the following day. Others go for 36 hours or only for a meal or two.

I encourage you to start out easy if you have never fasted before. It is important to fast when you know you have the time or can make the time. I do not recommend fasting while you are at work or are engaged in strenuous physical activity. If you do fast during those times, you may find yourself getting very fatigued and not being able to accomplish anything positive. If you have any medical concerns, speak to your doctor before deciding upon the type and length of a fast. Be reasonable and realistic. Examine your heart: God is not out to have you break the Guinness World Record for super-spirituality!

When you fast, you will become aware of the things that control you. Your stomach is programmed to have food put into it even when you do not need it and your mind has the habit of reminding you when you have missed a meal. Don't worry; you can miss a meal and not die of starvation. If you do eat something, don't condemn yourself. God doesn't. You can't prove anything to Him anyway. He loves you, wants to be with you and talk to you when you can give Him your undivided attention.

By: Pastor Bill Robison

A Way Of Life

Write what you learned about fasting and if you have decided to fast, what type of fast you will be doing and when you plan on starting:

CHAPTER 2

SILENCE AND SUBMISSION

This chapter is a continuation of all the previous book's chapters, combined. It is an earnest seeking for God in humble dependence. You can find Him in His Word and His creation, but what of when He speaks in "a still small voice" (1 Kings 19:12)?

SILENCE

When you listen in silence, He speaks. He wants you to listen, but you are likely often running around, listening to music or the TV and not stopping everything, especially your mind and heart. God says, "Be still, and know that I am God" (Psalm 46:10). This means to be still in your heart, mind and spirit. This scripture speaks to stop resisting and fighting (submission) against the Most High God and to have peace internally, knowing that He has His best for you. While stopping your body from running around is beneficial in spending quiet time with God, God can speak even when you are doing activities if you are seeking Him and even when you are not! The point is for your heart, mind and spirit to be quietly trusting God and wanting or waiting to hear from Him, regardless of what you are doing.

The more familiar you are with His voice the more often you will hear it. Even during chaos. Meeting frequently with the great "I am" is life changing. As you commune with the biggest lover of the universe, His love will flow through you in abundance! How joyful your heart will be as despair flees in His presence! How much bigger your worldview will be as you meet and spend time with Him.

Find a comfortable, consistent and convenient place and time to meet with Him without distractions. That is one of the most practical ways to fulfill the first part of the Golden Rule commandment which is loving God with all your heart, soul, mind and strength. Spend time with Him!

Your intellect can get in the way of hearing God and seeing His work in your life. The intellect is very important and necessary for understanding and applying God's Word to your life but if carried too far, analysis paralysis can harden your heart and emotions to God's touch. Going one step further, overanalyzing can keep you out of touch with your own emotions! How can you love yourself or the Lord your God with all your heart, mind, soul and strength if you are not aware of each area within yourself? How can you give yourself to your Maker (telling Him your feelings) if you do not know who and whose you are? How can you experience your Maker if you are not even open to experiencing yourself? This state of being is often referred to as "frozen" or "cut off at the neck," which means that emotions are not felt or if they are, the feelings are dismissed. There is a disconnect and the heart, emotions and the mind are not working together. Only the mind is working, making decisions alone and usually, they aren't what you really want.

How does analysis paralysis happen? Perhaps you were taught that emotions were not OK, so the ice began to build. Perhaps you made wrong choices and got hurt based on emotions and consequently decided not to listen to them at all. There are many possibilities, but your purpose here is not to delve into why but to give yourself permission to get to know yourself. This way, you can fully give your emotions and thoughts to God and hear His voice in silence.

This chapter is another tool by which you will sustain the progress made in previous ones. This chapter speaks to improving your conscious contact with the Trinity (God, the Father, God, the Son and God, the Holy Spirit). This requires discipline on your part. To know a friend, you spend time with him or her, right? The same applies to God. To know Him, you get to spend time with Him. Jesus knew that God knows best, so He spent time praying to God to know His will. The best example He gave us was when He prayed, "Not My will, but Your will be done" (Luke 22:42).

Our Lord also taught us to pray, saying, "Your will be done on earth as it is in heaven" (Matthew 6:10). To be able to pray like that sincerely, your heart belief would be that God is interested in all that you do and all that happens to you. You believe that He has your best interest at heart though you may not understand fully. Do you believe it? It's a choice to accept the truth that He loves you and is interested in you, so allow Him to work the feelings out if you are doubting. Tell Him about those feelings. Choose to believe and watch Him work! Additionally, making time for daily prayer and meditation will keep your growth moving forward by keeping you in close contact with God, through silence and submission.

THE HOLY SPIRIT

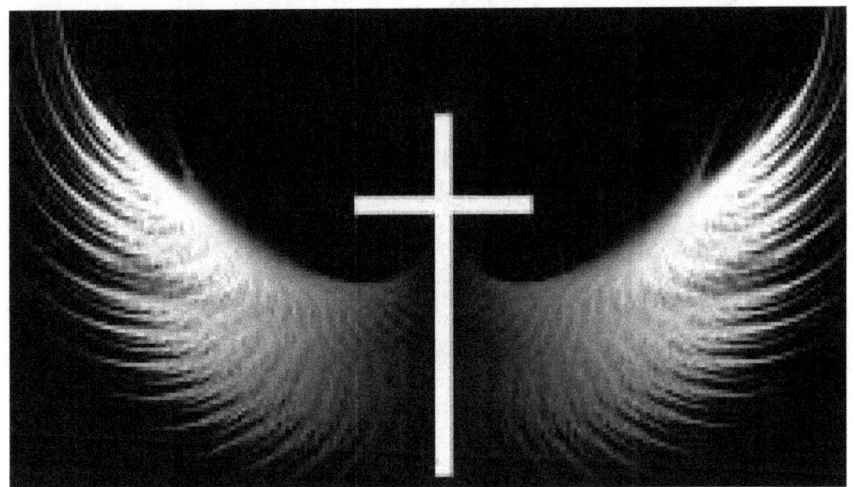

We have talked much about the Holy Spirit, but now we will study about Him in depth. R.A. Torrey states, in The Person and Work of the Holy Spirit (MI: Zondervan Publishing, 1974), that we must decide whether the "Holy Spirit is a divine Person, worthy of our adoration and our love; ... if He is some mysterious and wonderful power we can use; or who is a real person; holy, mighty and tender who is to get a hold of and use us" (pg.9).

Personality characteristics such as knowledge, feelings, will and teaching ability are ascribed to the Holy Spirit.

- Knowledge is ascribed to the Holy Spirit in 1 Corinthians 2:10-12, "But God has revealed them to us through His Spirit. For the Spirit searches all things, yes, the deep things of God. ..Even so, no one knows the things of God except the Spirit of God. ...we have received...the Spirit who is from God, that we might know the things that have been freely given to us by God."

- Delegating and will are ascribed to the Holy Spirit in 1 Corinthians 12:11, which states that the Spirit distributes "to each one individually as He wills."

- Romans 15:30 is about the Holy Spirit feeling, "the love of the Spirit." Ephesians 4:30 says not to grieve the Holy Spirit, another feeling

- John 14:26 states, "The Holy Spirit...will teach you all things," which shows the personality characteristic of impartation of knowledge through __*direct personal teaching*__

The Holy Spirit is indeed a Person, a distinct part of the Trinity, worthy to spend time with and learn of, as well as be praised and adored.

There are many jobs the Holy Spirit has that Scripture talks about; regeneration, the conviction of sin, guidance, searching and revealing, though that by no means encompasses all the works of the Spirit. Please refer to the suggested reading list and bibliography for more information on the Holy Spirit.

Spiritual regeneration is the impartation of spiritual life to those who are spiritually dead because of their sins. Jesus said, "It is the Spirit who gives life" (John 6:63). Being regenerated is being "born again, not of corruptible seed, but incorruptible, through the Word of God" (1 Peter 1:23). When the Holy Spirit convicts you of your sin from God's Word, and prompts you to receive Christ as your Lord and Savior, He comes to dwell within you permanently in your new life. Conversion is the change from Satan's camp, the dark, destructive evil side, to God's camp, the righteous, loving side. The outward manifestation of that internal work of regeneration is always evidenced by changed habits, changed lifestyles, joy and peace (to name a few).

The Holy Spirit is your guidance counselor into all truth (John 16:13-14) and reveals even the depths of God (1 Corinthians 2:10). Acts 13:2 tells us the Holy Spirit separated Paul and Barnabas for a specific work and sent them out. So too, He can send you out, "for we are His workmanship, created in Christ Jesus for good works, which God prepared that we should walk in them" (Ephesians 2:10). How exactly the Holy Spirit called Paul and Barnabas in Acts 13:2 is silent. It is the same with you in knowing God's will outside of what is clearly revealed in Scripture. He may make it known in one way and sometimes in another, but He will make His will known to you if you ask Him to. Additionally, He will never contradict God's Word. In other words, He won't give you an assignment or direction that is contrary to God's word (such as "Go murder this or that person"). Ask your Father in heaven, earnestly seek the answer and wait patiently upon the Lord for it (but serve until you hear specifics). Expect God to speak through His Word, others, or the Holy Spirit in that still, small voice. Listen closely and desire nothing other than to fulfill God's will. **An absolutely surrendered/submitted will is imperative for your mind to be clear in hearing God's will for you.** Otherwise, your will blocks you from hearing Him talk to you.

A block to surrendering your will could be fear. I remember a time when I became aware that I was a born-again Christian, I was afraid to submit myself to God as I thought He would send me to be a street preacher. I was so afraid! As I acknowledged this fear in me and talked to God about it, He showed me that if He called me to do that, He would change my heart and that I would want to share about Him on the streets. I have since done this very thing! God is a gentleman and I learned that *most* of the time, what He calls us to, He will prepare us and change our hearts to want to do what He has called us to do.

God also promises to provide all the guidance you need for every aspect of your life such as work, study, business and relationships. James 1:5-7 states, "If any of you lacks wisdom, let him ask God, who gives to all liberally and without reproach ... But let him ask in faith, with no doubting." So, ask, without doubting!

God says that the Holy Spirit *indwells* each believer who has accepted Jesus Christ as their Lord and Savior (at the time of salvation). *Being filled* by the Spirit is something else. Being filled by the Holy Spirit is the impartation of spiritual power (dunamis) for the sole purpose of testimony and service. You can have this by asking for it if you don't know whether you have it already. Being filled with the Spirit could be imparted to you when the Holy Spirit comes (or came) to dwell within you upon salvation or as a separate, empowering event. The important thing is to ask for it and believe that you have received it as it is His will for all believers to have this.

God tells us about His will in His Word and the infilling of the Holy Spirit gives us the ability to carry it out. Dwight L. Moody wisely stated, "Before we pray that God would fill us, I believe we ought to pray for Him to empty us [of our way]." So, pray that way and watch God work!

Being filled with the Spirit is a command (Ephesians 5:18), so it can't be something that happens only once and at salvation (accepting Jesus as our Lord and Savior). How are you filled with the Holy Spirit? "Let the Word of Christ dwell in you richly in all wisdom, teaching and admonishing one another in psalms, hymns and spiritual songs, singing with grace in your hearts to the Lord. And whatever you do in word or deed, do all in the name of the Lord Jesus, giving thanks to God the Father through Him" (Colossians 3:16-17). God's Holy Spirit flows in and through you to others when you worship, read, understand, are thankful, grateful and obey His Word.

Examples of walking with the spirit that I have experienced are:

1. Profession direction: When I was 17, suddenly there was a strong impression and knowing in my gut that I was to be a nurse. I applied to 3 nursing schools and was rejected by 2 of them. I figured that if the 3rd rejected me also, it wouldn't matter. I knew God would show me where to go as He told me, by the strong impression, to be a nurse. I knew that somehow, somewhere, I would be. I just didn't know how. I had no fear, worry, nor concern as I was submitted to Him and knew He was leading me ("Be still and know that I am God," Psalm 46:10). The 3rd nursing school accepted me and this profession has served me well throughout all the various seasons of my life.

2. Direction in my career: At one point, I was the supervisor of a dialysis nursing department and learned that the government was cutting the budget for dialysis. I looked at the department's expenses and the future incoming funds and knew that the department could not survive. I took this information to the nursing director who told me I was doing an excellent job and to keep on keeping on. They were even sending me to the East Coast to learn a new process. However, the Holy Spirit within me knew something was wrong and it was as if I was driving the bus with brakes on. I knew something was wrong. When I returned from the East Coast trip, the nursing director told me that they had sold the dialysis unit. I wasn't surprised! What the Holy Spirit had told me was true. The Holy Spirit then told me to wait...not to run around looking for another job but to wait, so I did. I watched and listened. Long story short, the dialysis unit closed on a Friday, and I started in the new Drug and Alcohol detox and recovery nursing unit my employer opened, on Monday. This work was born there. I also didn't

lose my seniority or benefits and didn't have to run around in chaos as I put myself in submission to God's leading. I could hear Him because I was listening, in submission. He is the good Shephard and led me to green pastures with and in peace!

3. There's another time (and many others) that I didn't listen to the Holy Spirit. At one point, I was young and naïve. I was picking up red flags with my fiancé, but did I talk to anyone about them? No, unfortunately, and I didn't know I was a Christian at this point of my life. I had also learned growing up that you don't talk about troublesome things. You only talk about good things. So, I didn't seek the Lord nor counsel from anyone wiser than myself and went through with the wedding. A month later, I found my husband kissing another woman. My ex-husband was not committed to me or to upholding his vows that he made before God, myself, and man. We later divorced. If I had sought wise counsel, I might have made a different choice.

The point about all the above is to seek God's wisdom. Seek this wisdom from reading the bible, seeking Godly counsel and sharing your life with other followers of Christ. He gives His wisdom liberally if you but ask. Therefore, go forth in the name of the Lord, knowing He has given you everything you need to finish the work He has called you to. Know that He will direct you! He made you to complete the works He ordained for you to walk in. Seek Him and your path will be known and shown to you. "Ask, and it will be given to you; seek, and you will find; knock, and it will be opened to you." (Matthew 7:7)

Scripture to memorize this week: Proverbs 23:12, "Apply your heart to instruction, and your ears to words of knowledge."

THE FLOW

The Holy Spirit dwells within you after you receive Christ as our Lord and Savior. Jesus said, "'If anyone thirsts, let him come to Me and drink. He who believes in Me, as the Scripture has said, out of his heart will flow rivers of living water.' But this He spoke concerning the Spirit, whom those believing in Him would receive" (John 7:37-39). This flow is the movement of love and God's Holy Spirit within you, directing and guiding your life as you listen to Him.

>The flow is within me,
>Yet I don't follow.

>I fear myself
>That I will not trust myself
>Enough to do what I hear.

>Yet if I don't do what I hear,
>It is wrong.
>What a backward way!

>But I know if I go with
>The flow, I will know.

>The fear is I may not
>Be able to control myself.
>That I will fall hard, care hard,
>Love hard. Is that so bad?

>It can be so good!

>*So, what am I afraid of?*

Intentionally decide to go with God's Holy Spirit though it may appear scary at first. He will lead and guide you into all truth and you can then stand on solid ground with truth as the solid foundation. You then, will not be moved or tossed to and fro.

What doubts do you still have that God knows and loves you?

What fears do you have that prevent you from receiving this knowledge emotionally?

How have you seen God answer your prayers during the last few weeks?

A Way Of Life

What has been your pattern of spending time with God daily?

What will you have to sacrifice to make time for God?

What changes would you want to make to spend more time alone with Him?

If you have done that already, what benefits have you received?

"O God, you are my God; early will I seek you," said the Psalmist (Psalm 63:1). If you follow his godly example, how much more will you have your antennae straight to hear God throughout the day. That will also help you set aside selfish motives resulting in better interaction patterns with others. How simple yet how hard to put into practice but practice makes almost perfect!

What fears do you have about the filling of the Holy Spirit and operating in the power of the Holy Spirit?

A Way Of Life

What don't you understand about this filling?

If you don't understand the above, please find someone who is well-versed in the Holy Spirit and who walks with God and in His power. Read the book, The Person and Work of the Holy Spirit (MI: Zondervan Publishing, 1974), listed in the bibliography. Remember daily to ask for forgiveness of your sins and the Holy Spirit will fill you up as you walk in obedience to God's way and His word. God will fill you, for He always keeps His word and delights in helping you obey all His commands if you are sincerely honest! In fact, "This is the confidence that we have in Him, that if we ask anything according to His will, He hears us [and in] whatever we ask [according to His revealed will], we know that we have the petitions that we have asked of Him" (1 John 5:14-15). If your heart attitude is right with God, ask whatever is according to His will, as revealed in His word and watch the Holy Spirit do much good through you!

CHAPTER 3

SHARING GOD'S KINGDOM PRINCIPLES WITH OTHERS

Another word for sharing God's kingdom principles with others is called discipleship. Discipleship is simply teaching others what you have been taught. It is following in the footsteps of the Holy Spirit. You are a comforter who comes alongside others to support them in sharing and applying God's kingdom principles to their lives.

Effective discipleship calls for supporting, not rescuing, or helping. Rescuing is being overly protective and doing the work for the other person because they don't know how or are thought to be inadequate. Rescuing prevents experiencing the consequences of actions taken and minimizes personal responsibility. The word "help" could give the *impression* that something is broken or that someone is incapable of doing something themselves and a person comes in and does a lot of the work. As such, rescuing and helping are not God's way. God's way is for each believer to grow towards and reach spiritual maturity, accepting responsibility for his or her own thoughts and actions. The spirit within the term support is assisting and encouraging the other person to be and do all that they were created to be and then, do. It is asking for permission to come and support the person to do what they are attempting to do; not come in, take over and do most of the work.

A Way Of Life

The following is a tool to assist you in determining where you are in the supporting versus rescuing/helping roles that you play in your life. It is beneficial to be reflective and completely honest in your personal appraisal. Regardless of where your score will fall, it's important to identify the role you play, most of the time, in relationships.

To the right of each statement, put a score code in the box. In the last row, total all your scores. The ___ stands for the significant others in your life: i.e., spouse, children, boss, parents, family, or friends.

SCORING CODE: 0 = seldom or never

   1 = sometimes or occasionally

   2 = frequently

1.	Is it hard for you to take time for yourself and have fun?	
2.	Do you supply words for ___ when he or she hesitates?	
3.	Do you set limits for yourself that you then ignore?	
4.	Do you believe you are responsible for making ___ happy?	
5.	Do you enjoy lending a shoulder for ___ to cry on?	
6.	Do you feel that others are not sufficiently grateful for your help?	
7.	Do you take care of others more than you take care of yourself?	

8.	Do you find yourself interrupting when ____ is talking?	
9.	Do you find it is difficult to say no to others?	
10.	Do you make excuses, openly or mentally, for ____?	
11.	Do you do more than your share or work harder than ____?	
12.	When ____ is unsure or uncomfortable about doing something, do you take over?	
13.	Do you give up doing things because ____ wouldn't like it?	
14.	Do you find yourself thinking that you know best for ____, than he or she does?	
15.	Do you think ____ would have grave difficulty getting along without you?	
16.	Do you use the word "we," and then find you don't have ____'s consent?	
17.	Do you stop yourself by feeling ____ will feel badly if you say or do something?	
18.	Is it hard for you not to respond to anyone who seems hurting or needs support even when he or she doesn't ask?	
19.	Do you find yourself giving advice that is not welcome?	
20.	Do you find yourself being resented when you were only trying to be helpful?	
21.	Is it easier to say "I'll do it myself" rather than delegate appropriately to others?	
	TOTAL	

ADD UP YOUR POINTS:

0-10 = minimum rescuing

11-19 = moderate rescuing

20 + = extensive rescuing

Where did your score fall? Regardless, it's good to look at how you relate to others. Now, let's look at the following examples of what support looks like vs. how a rescuer/helper responds.

The following is a comparison of the characteristics of both supporters and rescuers:

SUPPORTER	RESCUER/HELPER
1. Listens for request	1. Gives when not asked
2. Presents offer	2. Neglects to find out if the offer is welcome
3. Gives only what is needed	3. Gives help more and longer than needed
4. Checks periodically with the person	4. Omits feedback
5. Checks results: • functions better • meets goals • solves problems independently	5. Doesn't check results and feels good when accepted, but bad when turned down 6. Gets identity from helping 7. People pleaser

• uses suggestions successfully	

At times, you might feel good by being helpful while projecting your own needs onto others. You may be afraid to ask for what you really want, and the result is a compulsive helper who never quite feels satisfied. This is done from the position of "I'm OK; you're not OK, so I have to step in and help you because you're so inadequate." "Rescuers" usually wind up as victims and are often persecuted by those they were trying to rescue. Have you experienced this or responded to a helper or rescuer with irritation?

You can't change or support others unless they want to be changed or supported and then it is God who ultimately effects the change, not you. Truly supporting others can occur only when you are doing something for them that they desire and want. Giving support is more effective if you have been asked or received a "yes" if you asked whether support is wanted.

You may think that cultivating individual self-responsibility in others is selfish, uncaring, or callous. Initially, others may think ill of you as cultivating individual self-responsibility may not be part of the societal norm where you live. It is God's norm, though! Cultivating individual self-responsibility is a loving action and freedom is experienced by those who accept it.

Realize that you can most support others by going to God yourself, as you also point others to God. As He changes you, those around you will begin to respond to you differently. They must! You are different and as an effect, they change also.

To share God's way with others, you must first be a disciple of God. A disciple is one who follows another's teachings and ways and shares them with others. Obedience to His Word is key if you want His love and power to flow through you to others. Refer to the supporter characteristics and what you have been learning in the past weeks to reach out to others and teach them what you know of God's way. May God bless your efforts!

Scripture to memorize this week: 2 Timothy 2:2— "The things that you have heard from me among many witnesses, commit these to faithful men who will be able to teach others also."

What does God say about restoring your brother in Galatians 6:1, which says, "If a man is overtaken in any trespass, you who are spiritual, restore such a one in a spirit of gentleness, considering yourself lest you also be tempted," and how does that apply to discipleship?

What does God say, in Galatians 6:9— "Let us not grow weary while doing good, for in due season we shall reap if we do not lose heart," about the results of our discipleship labor?

What is God saying to you, in John 15:16— "You did not choose Me but I chose you, and appointed you that you should go and bear fruit..."

What fears do you have when you contemplate telling others what you have learned about God's way?

A Way Of Life

Notice what Deuteronomy 31:8 tells us about God: *"He is the One who goes before you. He will be with you; He will not leave you nor forsake you."* **How does that apply to your moving out in discipleship?**

Describe a recent scenario where you were telling someone what you have learned or are learning:

In knowing what to say as a disciple to others, notice what the Lord said to His most prominent disciple: "Who has made man's mouth? Or who makes the mute, the deaf, the seeing, or the blind? Have not I, the Lord? Now therefore, go, and I will be with your mouth and teach you what you shall say," Exodus 4:11. So even though you don't know everything, God can still use you if you are available and listening to His voice; not your own.

CHAPTER 4

SANCTIFICATION: PERSONAL GROWTH PLAN FOR ASSIMILATION & PRINCIPLE PRACTICE

Sanctification, according to Merriam-Webster, is defined as "the state of growing in divine grace as a result of Christian commitment after baptism or conversion." It is growing in grace and our emphasis is on the word, growing. This is not a stagnant walk, nor is it boring! But it is worth it. ☺ This principle was covered in depth in Book 2 but is covered again to look at applying the principles just reviewed.

I call a certain time in my life, baptism by fire. I was living in a marriage with my unfaithful husband and believed that God could change my marriage (which I do believe is the truth if BOTH parties are willing). So, I stayed in the marriage, hoping my husband would change his heart and mind. I knew that I was responsible for my part in the marriage, so began to pray that God would show me whatever I was doing wrong and change me. I asked God to create a clean heart in me and change my heart attitudes, motives and behaviors.

I went to God daily and asked Him to have His Holy Spirit search me. He began to show me gently what needed to be changed and as a gentleman, heal and clean my heart and teach me His ways. As I read the bible, I began to see how relationships and God's universal principles work and I became grateful and thankful for what He was showing me.

Look in the Appendix at the Dependence on God wheel. These are some sanctification steps and the first one is being willing. Therefore, be sincere and willing to become aware of what doesn't line up with God's ways through reading His word. Ask Him to change what He shows you and don't resist the change. You'll be changing from the inside out (instead of trying to "put the change on") and the change will stick. Do whatever action He says to do and don't worry or be scared, even if what you are learning is painful to admit or you don't completely understand, yet. God is a gentleman, and He will only collaborate with you to the point that you allow Him to. Do you want to be fully healed? Free from all your fears? Don't resist and seek the Lord. He will be with you 100% of the way. As you don't resist, you will gain as the following depicts:

"No pain, No gain."

These are the words the athletes sing
As they work their muscles to the sting.

"It hurts, it hurts," they cry
As the burning goes deeper and deeper into their thigh.

And yet they push on to never-ending fights,
Knowing that without this pain, they would never reach the heights.

And so, I say to you — you who so resist your pain —
Work it to the bone and do not deter,
For with your pain, you will gain.

—WHAT WE RESIST, PERSISTS—

PLAN

The intent of this book is the understanding and application of the information and principles covered, which is imperative for living victoriously. Below is a growth and development plan for you to utilize with the goal of solidifying these life-giving principles in your life and all the lives that this work touches.

To create a personal growth development plan, start by defining what you've learned and what you want your results to be. Make sure you write them down. Next, perform a self-assessment and identify one area from this book, that needs attention. Then, determine the required actions to effect the change and develop an action plan using the "SMARTER" goal-setting method, found in the appendix.

Here is an example of a growth plan:

What I want: To be effective as a leader of my family and at work.

What I do now:	What I learned:	What I will change:	The time period to practice my change:	The outcome:
I tend to control others and situations. I don't listen and make collaborative decisions with others.	I learned that surrendering frees me to be me. and that I don't have control over others. I only can control myself.	Listen with my heart before I speak. Listen for the truth and work with it only.	By the end of the next month.	1. My coworkers and family will notice and say something. 2. I will feel open on the inside rather than stressed and closed off.

Implement with goals: (see appendix on how to set goals)

Examples of SMARTER goals with its supporting activities to reach the stated goal:

Goal: By the end of next month, my family and coworker will see me as an effective leader as evidenced by them saying something about my behavior change and I will have a stress score reduction from an 8 to a 4 by the end of next month.

Specific:	yes (clear and simple)
Measurable:	stress score lower, family/coworkers will say something about my behavior change
Achievable:	this is achievable
Realistic:	this is realistic
Timely:	end of the next month
Evaluate goal:	end of next month and stress level reduction
Reset goal:	change it, extend the end time, or create another goal

Activities:

1. For the next month, at work and in every meeting, I will not be the first to speak and share my opinion. I will share...just not first!

2. For the next month, I will listen with my heart to what my family says and seek to understand their perspective before stating mine. I will do that by asking questions.

Now, it's your turn!

On a separate piece of paper that you can hang where you will see it frequently, type or write out your growth plan to assimilate and apply the principles you just learned. Find a safe friend who will listen and share your plan with them and as someone I know says, "git'r done!"

CONCLUSION

As A Way of Life, in its full workbook format, was so meaty, I was advised to divide the work into multiple small courses. Therefore, I have divided A Way of Life, Kingdom Principles for Living Victoriously, into 4 parts and this concludes Book 4. There is much more that leads to peace within and I want to encourage you to continue learning and applying God's principles so that you *will* experience freedom and peace within.

To continue your journey & in your internet browser, type in AWayofLifeMinistries.com. Click on the Bookstore or Courses tab to find resources and purchase whatever you need to continue your journey and growth. You can also search on Amazon for other titles by Nancy Williams and purchase them from there.

Please let us know how your journey is going by using the Contact Us form on the website to connect with us. We would LOVE to hear from you about how you are progressing. You can also subscribe to our blog page and we'll keep you informed of upcoming events, new publications, online courses, and book offerings. Hope to hear from you soon and if you have questions, please ask!

Blessings on your journey
~ Nancy ~

SUGGESTED READING LIST

The following 4 books are secular but may be helpful. Read them with caution and a biblically discerning mind.

- Beattie, Melody. (1987). Codependent No More. New York: Harper & Row.

- Bradshaw, John. (1988). The Family. Florida: Health Communications, Inc.

- Fromm, Erich. (1956). The Art of Loving. New York: Harper & Row.

- Peck, M. Scott, MD. (1978). The Road Less Traveled. New York: Simon & Schuster, Inc.

The following list is from a Christian perspective. I encourage you to read especially Francis Schaeffer's, True Spirituality, R.A. Torry's, The Person and Work of the Holy Spirit and J. Keith Miller's, A Hunger for Healing.

- Bennett, Dennis and Rita. (1971). The Holy Spirit and You. New Jersey: Logos International.

- Bridges, Jerry. (1978). The Pursuit of Holiness. Colorado: Navpress.

- Bridges, Jerry. (1983). The Practice of Godliness. Colorado: Navpress.

- Buhler, Rich. (1988). Pain and Pretending. Tennessee: Thomas Nelson, Inc.

- Esses, Michael. (1974). The Phenomenon of Obedience. New Jersey: Logos International.
- Huggett, Joyce. (1986). The Joy of Listening to God. Illinois: InterVarsity Press.
- Miller, J. Keith. (1991). A Hunger for Healing. New York: Harper Collins.
- Powell, John. (1969). Why Am I Afraid to Tell You Who I Am?. Illinois: Argus Communications.
- Powell, John. (1974). The Secret of Staying in Love. Texas: Argus Communications.
- Powell, John. (1976). Fully Human, Fully Alive. Illinois: Argus Communications.
- Powell, John. (1978). Unconditional Love. Texas: Argus Communications.
- Schaeffer, Francis A. (1971). True Spirituality. Illinois: Tyndale House Publishers.
- Seamands, David A. (1981). Healing for Damaged Emotions. Illinois: SP Publications, Inc.
- Smalley, Gary and Trent, John, Ph.D. (1986), The Blessing. Tennessee: Thomas Nelson, Inc.
- Smith, Chuck. (1979,1980). Effective Prayer Life. California: The Word For Today.
- Swindoll, Charles R. (1983). Dropping Your Guard. New York: Bantam Books.
- Torrey, R.A. (1974). The Person & Work of the Holy Spirit (rev. ed.). Michigan: Zondervan Publishing House.

- Watson, David. (1980). The Hidden Battle. Illinois: Harold Shaw Publishers.
- Whitfield, Charles L., M.D. (1987). Healing the Child Within. Florida: Health Communications, Inc.
- Wilkerson, David; and Sherrill, John & Elizabeth. (1963). The Cross and The Switchblade. New Jersey: Spire Books.

APPENDIX

It is recommended to review and use all the resources in this appendix to continue your growth journey and find your blessings as you do so.

USING A WAY OF LIFE IN GROUP SETTINGS	54
DEPENDENCE ON GOD	57
STRESS MANAGEMENT	59
THE SOCIAL READJUSTMENT RATING SCALE	67
TITHING	72
YEAR AT A GLANCE	76
YEAR AT A GLANCE – EXTRA BILLS	78
COMMUNICATION	80
GOAL SETTING	90
BIBLIOGRAPHY	96
ABOUT THE AUTHOR	101

USING A WAY OF LIFE IN GROUP SETTINGS

This book has been used in multiple group settings, so the below has been included to support group success and encourage individuals to be facilitators. Usually there is sharing of what God is doing in each person and what spoke to them from the chapter being reviewed.

GROUP LEADERS

Ground Rules, which are to be read to the small group:

- Confidentiality is of utmost importance
- Please don't put down another's person, thoughts, or opinions—each person is of equal value
- It's OK to say that you don't want to share
- Please share time equally. Give everyone a chance to share
- One person talks at a time
- Please be personal. Use "I" or "me" statements
- We work together as a team
- Talk from feelings, not stories or circumstances
- Don't give advice
- Listen and try to understand what is being said

Good Family Functional Rules taken from Bradshaw on: The Family by John Bradshaw. Copyright 1988. Health Communications, Inc.

A Way Of Life

Used with permission from the author and if used in the group, the group will be healthy. Facilitators are to read the following Functional Rules at the beginning of each group..

- Problems are acknowledged and resolved
- 5 freedoms—can be expressed and explored with no judgment:
    - perceptions
    - feelings
    - thoughts
    - desires
    - fantasies
- Communication is direct, specific and behavioral
- Family members get their needs met
- Family members can be different
- Parents do what they say (self-disciplined disciplinarians)
- Atmosphere is fun and spontaneous
- The rules require accountability
- Violation of another's values leads to guilt
- Mistakes are forgiven and viewed as learning tools
- Individuals are in touch with their healthy shame
- The family systems exist for each other

What to discuss in the group setting:

- What was particularly meaningful to you from the last chapter?
- How do you see this affecting your life right now?
- Are there any changes that you want to make?

Closing in Prayer: What can we pray about tonight or during this coming week?

DEPENDENCE ON GOD

See below, where God is in the middle and all the spokes have their focus on Him and His way. Walk through steps 1-11 in order and watch what happens within yourself! The result is having the change desired.

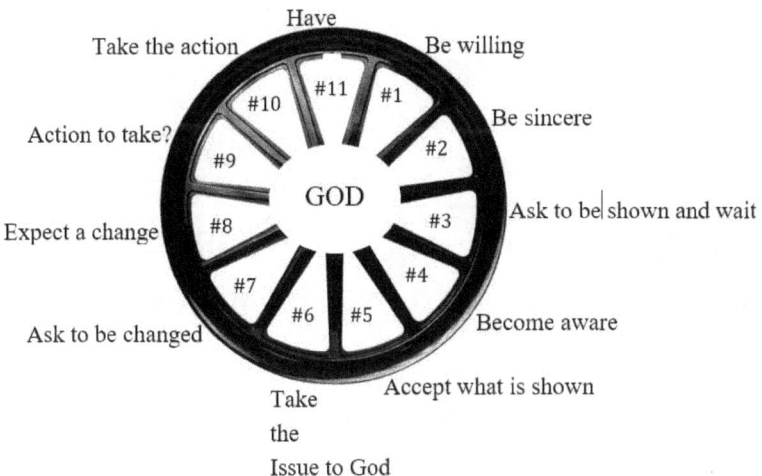

The beginning of your dependence on God starts with your being willing and goes until you BE, DO and then Have, regarding each situation. Be willing & sincere, ask to be shown and God will open your heart. You will begin to be aware of what you get to know. Accepting this knowledge is critical to your personal & spiritual growth. Take what God shows you back to Him and ask for it and for you to be changed. Expect Him to work within you and you will know when things are changing. He may show you some action to take, so make sure you complete the action, and you will be closer to being or having what He wants you to be or have.

This cycle works for everything and while most elements are important, being willing and sincere to ask to be shown what needs to be changed, or ask for understanding, etc. is most important. If you are not sincere or willing, this cycle of growth and understanding will not work.

Point # 1	You are WILLING
Point # 2	You are SINCERE
Point # 3	You ASK TO BE SHOWN
Point # 4	You are AWARE
Point # 5	You ACCEPT WHAT WE ARE SHOWN
Point # 6	You TAKE THE ISSUE TO GOD
Point # 7	You ASK TO BE CHANGED
Point # 8	You EXPECT A CHANGE
Point # 9	You look for what ACTION TO TAKE
Point # 10	You TAKE THE ACTION
Point # 11	You BE, DO, then HAVE

To refresh the understanding of what is meant by the BE—DO—HAVE statement, refer to the introduction at the beginning of this book. Then, enjoy and experience the newfound freedom that God gives to you as you submit and depend on Him!

STRESS MANAGEMENT

Stress is an ever-present reality. You may thrive on or even create more stress in your life, while others run from any kind of stress. It can be either positive or negative and the key to managing your stress in a healthy way is the tools you use to cope with it.

Stress is any strain or pressure on the body or mind. A stressor is that which causes stress. Distress is a state of mental or physical anguish. It can also be the result of mismanaged stress. Recognizing the kind of stress you are under, as well as your usual response to stress, is how you begin managing or lessening the stress effects on your body, mind and life.

PHYSICAL SYMPTOMS OF DISTRESS:

Anxiety	Churning stomach	Depression
Edginess	Poor concentration	Short-temperedness
Irritability	Accelerated speech	Tight shoulders
Sore back	Fuzzy thinking	Hand trembling

There may be other symptoms that your body manifests. Write these in the space provided:

The above symptoms are some of the early warning signs that something is wrong and needs to be changed. Doctors estimate that 80 percent of illnesses are stress related. The following are sometimes the manifestations of chronically ignored stress (by no means indicating that if you have one of these diseases, it was necessarily because of chronic stress):

Ulcers	Heart attacks
Cancer	Rheumatoid arthritis
High-blood pressure	Dizziness
Migraine headaches	Chronic back pain
Colitis	Non-cardiac pain

Your performance level can give you a hint of your stress level. If you are too busy and do not have time to carry out your normal responsibilities, your body will let you know. Your energy level will begin to drop, and your focus will begin to wane. You may also feel guilty about not taking care of your responsibilities which will also zap your energy. Conversely, not having enough stress in your life can be as bad as having too much. It all depends on the type of stress and how you cope with it.

INDICATORS OF IDEAL STRESS LEVEL

High-energy level	Thorough analysis of problems
Mental alertness	Improved memory and recall
High motivation	Sharp perception
Calmness under pressure	Optimistic outlook

INDICATORS OF UNDER-STRESS OR OVER-STRESS

Boredom	Fatigue
Apathy	Insomnia
High accident rate	Change in appetite
Frequent grievances	Negative outlook
Absenteeism	Errors/indecisiveness
Increased use of drugs, alcohol, food, or tobacco	

FIGHT-OR-FLIGHT RESPONSE

When stress enters, your baseline stress level rises and then falls with the resolution of the stress. If your stress is chronic, your baseline starts higher and with more stress, but does not fall back to its original, normal level due to the chronic stress. That taxes the chemical structure of your body on an ongoing basis, with the eventual breakdown somewhere in your mind or body.

MANAGING STRESS

An integrated approach to managing stress is vital to the proper care of the person God made you to be.

EQUIPPING YOUR SPIRIT

From what I have seen in my life and by observing others, the primary cause of negative stress (distress) is the desire for control. Prayer is a wonderful remedy, as it brings us before our Father in our rightful place of submission as His children. When we "seek first the kingdom of God and His righteousness" (Matthew 6:33), control ceases to be important. I have felt the tension leave me as I tell Him of my concerns and struggles and leave them in His hands while seeking what steps I'm to take in any situation.

EQUIPPING YOUR MIND

Taking time each day to relax and allow your body to quiet down is important for turning off the fight-or-flight response. Learning to set limits and saying no to external and internal demands reduces your stress. What about the demands of your phone notifications? Have you thought about turning them off? Jesus said to His disciples, "Come aside...and rest awhile" (Mark 6:31). You can take periodic rest and renewal to keep yourself at peak efficiency. Rest also helps you to regroup and focus. To make sure you are going in the direction your Maker intends you to go rather than aimlessly being active. Bringing all thoughts into the captivity of Jesus (2 Corinthians 10:5) will enable you to determine what voice you are hearing. If it does not line up with God's Word, the voice may be your flesh or Satan's.

Another helpful scripture to monitor your mind, so you can bring thoughts into captivity (put the negative doubt-filled thoughts in jail and lock the door), is Philippians 4:8, which states, "Whatever things are true...noble...just...pure...lovely...of good report; if there is any virtue, and if there is anything praiseworthy—think on these things." Applying this scripture is the death of thoughts such as "I'm no good," "No one loves me," or, "I'm a failure." God says to "be transformed by the renewing of your mind" (Romans 12:2—i.e., to look and see what I, God, think of you and for you to know how much I love you). Learning and accepting how God thinks, loves and promises to act towards you is key to winning the battle of the mind. It is a conscious battle. To win, you must take responsibility for disciplining your own thoughts and train them in the way they should go (God's way and in faith). Your stress level will thank you!

EQUIPPING YOUR BODY

Regular physical exercise is important for several reasons, including:

- Healthy outlet for stored energy
- Increases circulation and improves body functions
- Increases production of endorphins for feelings of well-being
- Increases muscle tissue

Regular exercise keeps your body strong so that at times of strain, you will not hurt yourself. Regular exercise raises your metabolism rate by increasing muscle tissue, which burns calories more efficiently than fat tissue. Fad diets do not work so if your goal is to lose weight, increase your amount of exercise and cut down the greasy fried fat content of the food you are eating. Over time, if you are consistent, your weight will start to drop. For women, regular exercise that places stress on the long bones helps build them up and counteracts the effects of osteoporosis.

In looking at stress management, you may not even consider what you do to your body when you consume the foods that you eat. How does your body react to certain foods? How hard does your body have to work to digest one food over another? Is your mind clearer when you eat certain foods than others? Caffeine and sugar play a major part in increasing stress. Caffeine stimulates your kidneys and if consumed in excess, can cause increased nervous symptoms. Caffeine also depletes the body of your stress vitamins by increasing your urinary output and as Vitamins B and C are water-soluble, they are excreted through the kidneys via urine. The question is, are you replacing them in times of higher stress?

Eating a high-sugar diet also depletes the stress vitamins in your body (Vitamins B and C), while shocking your pancreas when a load of sugar is pumped into the bloodstream. As the pancreas responds with a release of insulin, if no protein is around to stabilize the blood sugar, the blood sugar will initially shoot up and you might feel a rush of energy. A short time later, because of the amount of insulin released, your blood sugar will drop, and you can become listless, tired and depressed. So, you eat or drink again and the roller coaster continues. Two excellent books for more information on nutrition are The Nutrition Almanac (NY: McGraw-Hill, 1993) and Dr. Roger T. Williams Nutrition Against Disease (NY: Pitman Publishing, 1971).

Other stress-management tools include:

- Social support—Allow family, friends, church and neighbors to lend stability, guidance and caring to your life. Strength flows from giving as well as receiving

- Anchors—Be faithful in following your religious and personal beliefs, establish sensible daily routines and identify a few favorite spots in nature both near and far that you like to spend time at:

- Physical care—Continue good health and fitness habits during both good and bad times. Make priorities of eating well, exercising and relaxing

- Involvement—Get involved. Active participation in the community, church and political affairs adds to a sense of belonging and contribution to others. Don't wait for others to come to you—go to them

- Perception—Have God's worldview, as well as God's perception of who you are: His valued child

- Reactions to distress—Make choices and decisions in a timely manner with godly counsel rather than ignoring the issues you know you need to face

The ways you normally react to stress are:

The area in your life with the most stress is:

You want to make the following changes in your lifestyle:

You will incorporate these tools by (what activities you will do):

THE SOCIAL READJUSTMENT RATING SCALE

Drs. Thomas Holmes and Richard Rahe of the Department of Psychiatry at the University of Washington School of Medicine developed the Social Readjustment Rating Scale. This scale, originally published in the Journal of Psychosomatic Research Volume 11 (1967), is reprinted with permission from Elsevier Science Ltd., Pergamon Imprint, Oxford, England and lists forty-three life events along with a corresponding value. A person's score on this scale can be useful in predicting that person's chances of becoming ill or having an accident in the next two years. **A score of 150 to 299 indicates approximately a 50% chance; a score of above 300 indicates approximately a 90% chance of becoming seriously ill or injured in the next two years.** This research indicates a strong correlation between stress and illness but also illustrates that people react differently to stressors. If stressors alone caused illness, then 100% of those with high scores would become ill. If you have a high score on this scale, that doesn't mean you are going to become ill. It means it's time to use your resources and strengths to minimize your chances and take extra good care of yourself.

To use this rating scale, add the value of each life event that applies to you within the last year and total your score.

LIFE EVENT	SCORE
Death of a spouse	100
Divorce	73
Marital separation	65
Jail term	63
Death / family member	63
Personal injury/illness	53
Marriage	50
Fired at work	47
Marital reconciliation	45
Retirement	45
Health	44
Pregnancy	40
Change in family members	39
Sex difficulties	39
Gain of new family member	39
Business readjustment	39
Change in financial state	38
Death of a close friend	37
Change of Line of work	36
Change in number of arguments with spouse	35

Mortgage or loan. A major purchase	31
Foreclosure of mortgage or loan	30
Change in responsibility at work	29
Son or daughter leaves home	29
Trouble with in-laws	29
Outstanding personal achievement	28
Begin or end school	26
Wife begins or stops work	26
Change in living conditions	25
Revision of personal habits	24
Trouble with the boss	23
Change/work hrs./conditions	20
Change in residence	20
Change in schools	20
Change in recreation	19
Change in church activities	19
Change in social activities	18
Mortgage/Loan for a lesser purchase	17
Change in sleeping habits	16

Change in eating habits	15
Change in # of family get-togethers	15
Vacation	13
Minor violation of the law	11
TOTAL:	

What other events can you think of in your life that are not listed in this scale and that took significant energy for you to adjust to?

What coping skills do you see already incorporated in your life?

A Way Of Life

What coping skills do you plan to incorporate into your life and how do you plan to do that?

TITHING

In seeking to be good stewards of the finances God has given you, there's a question to start with: What is tithing and what is taught about it in Scripture?

The term "tithe" means a tenth and yet it is hardly the last word on all God's principles regarding giving. Here is a basic summary using the following scriptures taken from the Old Testament:

- Genesis 28:22—Jacob said to God, *"Of all that You give me, I will surely give a tenth [tithe] to You."*

- Leviticus 27:32— *"Concerning the tithe of the herd...the tenth one shall be holy to the Lord."* The tithe was a part of the Levitical law given to the nation of Israel

- Ecclesiastes 5:4-5— *"When you make a vow to God, do not delay to pay it.... Better not to vow than to vow and not pay."*

- Proverbs 3:9,10— *"Honor the Lord with your possessions, and with the first fruits of all your increase; So your barns will be filled with plenty, and your vats will overflow with new wine."* In this scripture, God promises blessings with your giving

The following scriptures are taken from the New Testament:

- Matthew 6:1-4— *"Do not do your charitable deed before men, to be seen by them.... Do...in secret; and your Father who sees in secret will Himself reward you openly"*

- Matthew 25:14-30—These scriptures talk about the parable of the talents, which teaches that you are to return to the Lord the increase of your work. For example, whatever investment returns you receive, whatever pay increases you are given, you are to return some portion to the Lord. These are financial examples, but this also applies to your spiritual giftings. All you are and have come from God and you are called to be good stewards of any gifts given. All these gifts were His first anyway before He gave them to you and you get to use them for His glory. Remember, you are to give cheerfully and not grudgingly or out of duty, as the decision of what to give, comes from the heart

- Acts 5:1-11—These scriptures talk about the account of Ananias and Sapphira, who lied to the Holy Spirit about the amount they gave to the Lord's work and dropped dead due to their lying. We are never to lie to God and others about our giving or about anything

- 1 Corinthians 16:1— *"Concerning the collection for the saints...on the first day of the week let each one of you lay something aside, storing up as he may prosper"*

- 2 Corinthians 8:10-15—These scriptures cover the purpose of giving; that there may be basic equality—that those who have abundance share with those who have little so every believer's needs are met

- 2 Corinthians 9:7— *"Let each one give as he purposes in his heart, not grudgingly or of necessity; for God loves a cheerful giver"*

In the New Testament, there is not a Levitical law that demands a tenth of your wage. God looks for the believer that purposes in his heart about what to give and does it cheerfully without grumbling.

A tenth, however, is a good, simple figure to start from, and God will lead you from there. Beware of selfish thinking regarding giving: God will not automatically increase your reward financially tenfold, but He does promise blessings. He could give you an increase in other ways but the heart of your giving is not to get something back from God. It is recognizing that the possessions and money you have are all His anyway and that you have been given stewardship over what He has given or will give you.

An example of this is when I was suddenly single and had to budget and pay my bills while working a part-time job. I talked to God and promised Him that I would increase what I gave back to Him on a scheduled basis (purposed in my heart) and proceeded to increase my giving accordingly. Now being married, we continue to do so and God has been our faithful provider as we have been faithful givers.

God says, in 1 Timothy 5:17-18, to give double honor to the elders, "especially those who labor in the Word and doctrine. For the Scripture says…'the laborer is worthy of his wages.'" Clearly, you are to pay the church (donations) for those who labor, especially those who teach God's Word.

The heart of God is for you to decide what to give right away, not basing your giving on what is left over at the end of the week. That way, He has your heart and money, and your money does not own you. God does not want you to be in bondage to your money but to exercise good stewardship. As you put Him first, you are free. Keep in mind that giving is not only about money but also giving of your time and gifts to the Body of Christ.

Let's assume that you are going to give a tenth of your income to the Lord's work. Do you tithe on your net (after-tax dollars) or on your gross (before-tax) income? The Bible is silent on that account. It does say to "render to Caesar the things that are Caesar's, and to

God the things that are God's" (Mark 12:17), but that does not answer the above question precisely. Those who advocate tithing on the after-tax dollars (net income), point out that the taxes paid to the government never come under your "stewardship control", so were never yours in the first place. Those advocating tithing on our pre-tax dollars tend to operate on the adjusted gross income which is that remaining after adding in interest while deducting business expenses, inventory and losses. But does this really matter?

The important principle here is that God wants you to be a cheerful giver, determining in your own heart what to give. It could be more than a tenth of your gross income! So, pray about what you are to give and study God's word regarding giving. You may be in a place where you would not be able to feed your family if you tithed, so do not let this burden you. God wants your heart, so make a commitment to a giving plan with gradual increases as God enables and guides you. You can also seek counsel from your pastor if you have one.

YEAR AT A GLANCE

The following pages are to help you plan for your monthly bills and extra bills that come in at approximately the same time each year which can help you plan your finances. Read the following, and then proceed with filling out the pages (or their equivalent, such as using a spreadsheet computer program).

On the page listed 12-MONTH FINANCIAL PLANNER for Routine Bills, list the monthly or every-other-month bills you pay. That includes credit cards, telephone, gas, electric and rent or mortgage payments. In the months provided, write in the amount (or approximate amount) of the bill. Add each column to obtain a monthly total, and then add each monthly total to obtain a yearly total. Next, take your yearly total and divide that number by the number of paychecks you receive per year. That number is the amount you are to put aside each paycheck to pay all your **routine** bills as they come in each month.

YEAR AT-A-GLANCE—12-MONTH FINANCIAL PLANNER FOR ROUTINE BILLS

Month	Gas	Water	Phone	Rent / Mortgage	Medical Insurance	Life Insurance	Car Payment	Credit Card	Monthly Total
Jan.									
Feb.									
Mar.									
April									
May									
June									

A Way Of Life

July								
Aug.								
Sept.								
Oct.								
Nov.								
Dec.								

FORMULA: Yearly total divided by number of paychecks = amount to save per paycheck.

    Yearly total: Amount to save per paycheck: _____

YEAR AT A GLANCE – EXTRA BILLS

In the next table, list bills such as homeowner's insurance, car insurance, DMV, car maintenance approximation, real-estate taxes, subscriptions to magazines, health club membership if not monthly and any other bill that comes less than every two months. In the months provided, write in the amount (or approximate amount) of the bill. Add each column to obtain a monthly total, and then add each monthly total to obtain a yearly total.

Next, take your yearly total and divide that by the number of paychecks you receive per year. That is the amount you are to put aside each paycheck to pay all your **extra bills** as they come in throughout the year.

Some individuals set up a separate savings account for these bills, while others use envelopes in the home for the same purpose. Where you decide to keep extra money is best determined by whether you are tempted to spend it if it is readily available. For instance, if available, a four-month CD that is set aside every month for real estate taxes cannot be touched until it matures. If you set it up to mature every March, August and November, you have the money available to use in time to pay your two tax installments (if you live in CA) in April and December. The point is that you will have the funds available without stress, as you planned for and set the funds aside.

If you think you can keep the extra money at home safely, you have the advantage of having the cash available should you need to borrow from it with the intent that you promptly pay the envelope back at your next paycheck. It's your money to do with as you will with the goal of being prepared and having the funds available to pay these bills. Doing this will lessen the chaos and stress in your life.

YEAR AT A GLANCE-12 MONTH PLANNER FOR EXTRA BILLS

Month	Car Insurance	Magazine subscription	Property Tax				Monthly Total
Jan.							
Feb.							
Mar.							
April							
May							
June							
July							
Aug.							
Sept.							
Oct.							
Nov.							
Dec.							

FORMULA: Yearly total divided by number of paychecks = amount to save per paycheck.

Yearly total: _____   Amount to save per paycheck: _____

COMMUNICATION

The following depicts key elements of the communication process. They are given in outline fashion to make it easy for you to review them often, for the more you understand and practice them, the more your communication with others will improve.

Communicate with purpose:

- Influence behavior/ideas/thoughts
- Convey information
- Build relationships

Before communicating, ask yourself if your purpose is to confront, resolve an issue, or share since the way you approach speaking will differ. Remember a key biblical concept: Philippians 2:3— "Let nothing be done through selfish ambition or conceit, but in lowliness of mind let each esteem others better than himself." Applying that scripture to your attitude and heart as you communicate will support your awareness of how words may be perceived by others and how that affects their feelings.

Ways of communicating:

- Linear-----one sided

    Person A sends a message to person B

    (sender-------->--------->receiver)

- Circular

    Person A sends a message to B and B responds. Feedback happens

    Sender A <--------------->B receiver and then B sends a communication back to sender. Communication doesn't continue. Example: A: How are you? B: I'm fine

- Mutual transaction

    Person A sends a message to B and B responds. A then responds

    A----->B----->A----->B

    Feedback happens both ways with increased emotional relating (both influence the other)

You as a sender:

- Must be clear in the message sent
- Responsible to evaluate the *words used to send the message* and if what was said was exactly what you wanted to send

You as a receiver:

- Responsible to understand that you *hear through your perception filter*, which can result in a *different message heard than what was sent*
- You are responsible for verifying that what you heard is what was sent, by the sender

Be aware that receivers can have preconceived ideas of the sender, which will cloud communication. The mutual transaction helps ensure that what was said was heard correctly. *Verifying that what you received is what was meant to be sent is the key to preventing misunderstandings and assumptions.*

Non-verbal communication:

Non-verbal communication comprises about 55 percent of the communication process. The rest of the breakdown is 7 percent verbal, 38 percent vocal, with inconsistencies in what you say and do frequently occurring.

In Non-verbal communication:

a. Our 5 senses are used: Sight, hearing, smell, taste, touch

b. 4 categories

- Kinesics—your body movements, facial expressions, body language, clothes
- Tactile—who can touch whom, when and how
- Paralanguage—how your voice is when speaking (tone—which includes the force of your voice; if your voice is relaxed or edgy, etc.)
- Proxemics
    - Use of physical/personal space
    - Who can come in and when
    - Distance
        - public—no personal contact
        - social—4-12 feet
        - personal—1½ -4 feet
        - intimate—6"-18"

c. More feelings are communicated non-verbally than verbally

Factors affecting how communication is perceived:

   a. Our mood

   b. Preconceived notions of the speaker and the topic being spoken about (selective hearing)

   c. Mental level of the person being spoken to

Evaluating your communication:

   a. Speaker—primary responsibility to get ideas across
   - Emotions can cloud the words used
   - Emotions cloud the way words are used
   - Pushing past emotion, speak accurately and lovingly
   - Stay focused and avoid distractions

   b. Hearer—keep in mind:
   - Distractions
   - Vocabulary and language skills
   - Wishful hearing
   - Perception filter

   c. Things to avoid in your communication:
   - Using clichés
   - Giving unwanted advice or approval
   - Belittling speech or actions
   - Disagreeably disagreeing

- Being defensive
- Stereotyping and over-generalizing
- Changing the subject before resolution such as bringing up other topics that don't relate and can throw off the focus (if allowed) of the topic being discussed
- Blaming
- Responding with anger and hostility—Proverbs 17:14 says, "The beginning of strife is like a releasing [a flood]. Therefore, stop contention before a quarrel starts."
- Raising more than one issue at a time
- Judging (condemning) —Matthew 7:2— "With what judgment you judge, you will be judged."

Tools for excellent, honest communication:

a. Active listening—we speak about 125 words per minute but think about 4 times as fast

- Demonstrate understanding and respect for the speaker's message and feelings
- Be empathetic and sympathetic
- Concentrate on the speaker's perspective
- Is not casual—takes energy
- Is not parroting back words, but using open-ended questions, such as, "Can you give me an example?"
- Is a priority: James 1:19 says, "Let every man be swift to hear, slow to speak, slow to wrath."

b. Considerate speaking:
   - Raise only one issue at a time
   - "Be kind to one another, tenderhearted to one another, just as God in Christ forgave you" (Ephesians 4:32)
   - "A soft answer turns away wrath, but a harsh word stirs up anger" (Proverbs 15:1)
   - Proverbs 16:21 says, "The wise in heart will be called prudent and sweetness of the lips increases learning."

c. Clarification:
   - Attempt to understand
   - *Validate what a person is saying*
   - Focus
   - *Summarize to make sure what was said was indeed heard*

d. Be aware of others and your nonverbal body language (see following pages)

e. Follow the speaker. What this means is to listen to the whole story. Don't judge or tune out as you may miss an important idea, a person's heart, their point, or something about the person sharing. Jesus told His disciples to follow and learn of Him; to learn of His perspective. With an open mind and listening skills, you can walk alongside others, learn their perspective and love them

Concluding scriptural consideration: Philippians 4:8 says to meditate on whatever is:

- True
- Noble
- Just
- Pure
- Lovely
- Of good reputation (or good report)
- Virtuous
- Praiseworthy

God calls you to cultivate an attitude of thinking the best for all and facilitating the best in all. Your flesh wants you to assume the worst, even though the worst may not exist except in your own mind because of your past. God calls you not to think about those things but on the best, so training your mind is the ongoing task.

Non-verbal behavioral components:

Type	Aggressive	Assertive	Passive
Eye contact	Stares, glares	Looks in eyes	Avoids eyes
Posture	Exaggerated, rigid	Open, upright	Slumped, head down
Gestures	Tightly clenched fist, points finger	Relaxed, expressive	Fidgeting hands
Distance	Intrusive	Comfortable	Moves away
Verbal loudness	Louder than the normal range	Normal range	Softer than the normal range

Tone of voice	Harsh	Clear	Clear to sing-song/whiny
Style/fluency	Offensive, bombastic	Direct, smooth	Indirect, interrupts
Content	Derogatory put-downs	To the point, brief	Wordy, indirect
Listening	Interrupts and is closed to other's viewpoint	Doesn't interrupt when others speak. Listens to others' viewpoints, open	Tendency is to partially listen to what is said & often misinterprets

Basics of good communication:

a. Active listening

b. Open questioning

c. Accepting and reflecting feelings

Activity	Examples of Activity
Active Listening: Convey interest in what the other person is saying	Smiling, nodding, eye contact, "I see", "uh-huh"
Encourage the other to expand further	"Yes, go on," "Tell me more," "I'd like to hear more"
Open Questioning: Help the other clarify the problem in their thinking. Help the other hear what they have said in the way it sounded to you. Pull out the key ideas	"Then the problem as you see it is that..." "If I understand you correctly, you are saying that..." "Your major concern is..."
Accepting and reflecting feelings: Respond to the other's feelings more than their words	"You feel strongly that..."

OFFERING CONSTRUCTIVE COMPLIMENTS:

- Be specific—focus on behavior or incident
- Be direct
- Compliment in public
- Compliment often but be sincere and sensitive

Offering constructive criticism:

- Be specific—focus on a behavior or incident
- Be sure the behavior you are criticizing can be changed
- Talk from your own point of view, and avoid threats and accusations
- Don't belabor the point
- Offer incentives for changed behavior and commit yourself to share in resolving the situation
- Empathize with the other's problem or feelings
- Choose an appropriate time and place

Accepting compliments:

- Say thank you!

Accepting criticism:

- Think of it as a source of new information to be evaluated objectively
- Channel the emotional energy aroused by criticism into fruitful avenues

- Take the necessary steps to put behavioral changes into action

The above talks about how to create good communication, regardless of how the other responds. Your responsibility is how you communicate. How the other person you are communicating with communicates back is not your responsibility and you get to separate yourself to that truth. In other words, don't REACT if the other person is not responding in the same manner as what you have been learning. It takes time but the more you do your responsibility and not attempt to control the outcome, the better your communication will be regardless of how a person responds back.

There are three books I would like to recommend in support of improving your communication style. The information for these books can also be found in the appendix and they are:

1. Boundaries, by Henry Cloud and J. Townsend
2. Am I Making Myself Clear, by Terry Felber
3. The 16 Undeniable Laws of Communication, by John C. Maxwell

GOAL SETTING

Many individuals have never been taught about goal setting. This exercise will teach you how to clearly state your goals and then set up subgoals (activities) to achieve them.

First—why should you set goals? Isn't God supposed to do everything for you? He can intervene and move you where He wants you to be, can't He? So, why do you have to do anything?

Yes, God can move you if He so desires to work that way. Most often, He doesn't. He can speak to you, but it is up to you to function as His vessel here on earth as He didn't make us puppets. Setting goals can be for any part of your life—for what God has spoken to your heart for you to do, for your own growth, education, or fun.

When goals are set, there's something that will arise in you to begin working to complete the goal. A purpose will grow within you and just skimming along in life doing who knows what, ends. Goals don't have to be great feats, but as you begin setting goals and moving forward, God directs your path. You can direct a moving car, but not a parked car. Goals help you get moving!

Think of the term SMARTER to support you in writing your goals:

Specific (make it simple and clear)

Measurable

Achievable

Realistic

Timely

Evaluate

Reset goal

Sample Goal:

I will study my Bible 4 times a week for 1 hour over a one-month period, in June.

S:	personal Bible study
M:	4 times/week
A:	clearly stated
R:	can be achieved
T:	over a month's time (specify which month)
E:	to be done after a month's time or throughout the month
R:	select another month or pick different Bible-study goals

Subgoals (or activities) are those behaviors or specific activities you must do to achieve your expected end. Using the goal example above, activities might include:

- setting the alarm earlier
- choose the place and time for Bible study
- not planning anything else for that time frame
- turning phones and TVs off

You can be as creative as you want to be.

On the following pages, write down goals that you want to incorporate in your life and the subgoals or activities needed to achieve them, using the SMARTER way of setting goals.

LIFE DOMAIN GOALS

Life Domains (adjust the following to your needs)

SPIRITUAL GOALS: Activities

HEALTH AND FITNESS: Activities

JOB: Activities

A Way Of Life

EDUCATION: Activities

SOCIAL/FAMILY: Activities

RECREATION: Activities

FINANCIAL: Activities

List an area of your life and write down where you see God leading you in that area within the next year, 5 years and 10 years. You can repeat setting these goals with any area of your life. If you do not have any direction right now, seek the Lord and begin to make plans but be ever watchful in case you are going off His path for you. He will let you know and guide you as you move out. Proverbs 16:9 states, "A man's heart plans his way, but the Lord directs his steps."

Proverb 16:3 promises, that when you "commit your works to the Lord, your thoughts will be established." How wonderful to know that He will give you clear and solid thoughts as you trust and obey Him!

Area:

1 year:

5 years:

10 years:

BIBLIOGRAPHY

Andrews, Andy. (2002). The Traveler's Gift. Tennessee: Thomas Nelson, Inc.

Beattie, Melody. (1987). Codependent No More. New York: Harper & Row.

Bender, Stephanie & Keleher, Kathleen. (1991). PMS—A Positive Program to Gain Control. New York: The Body Press.

Bennett, Dennis & Rita. (1971). The Holy Spirit and You. New Jersey: Logos International.

Berkhof, Louis. (1933). Manual of Christian Doctrine. Michigan: William B. Eerdmans Publishing Company.

Bradshaw, John. (1988). The Family. Florida: Health Communications, Inc.

Bridges, Jerry. (1978). The Pursuit of Holiness. Colorado: Navpress.

Bridges, Jerry. (1983). The Practice of Godliness. Colorado: Navpress.

Buhler, Rich. (1988). Pain and Pretending. Tennessee: Thomas Nelson, Inc.

Burkett, Larry. (1990). The Financial Planning Workbook. Chicago: Moody Press.

Campbell, Roderick. (1954). Israel and the New Covenant. Pennsylvania: Presbyterian and Reformed Publishing Company.

Cloud, H., & Townsend, J. (1992). Boundaries. Michigan: Zondervan Publishing House.

Corey, Gerald F. (1977). Theory and Practice of Counseling and Psychotherapy (2nd ed.). California: Wadsworth.

Dileo, Sandy. (1984). "Stress Management". California: Author.

Edman, V. Raymond. (1948). The Disciplines of Life. Minnesota: World Wide Publication.

Elwell, Walter A. (Editor). (1989). Evangelical Commentary on the Bible. Michigan: Baker Book House.

Engstrom, Ted W. (1976). The Making of a Christian Leader. Michigan: Zondervan Publishing House.

Erickson, Millard J. (1985). Christian Theology. Michigan: Baker Book House.

Esses, Michael. (1974). The Phenomenon of Obedience. New Jersey: Logos International.

Felber, Terry. (2002), Am I Making Myself Clear? Nashville: Thomas Nelson.

Foster, Richard. (1992). Prayer—Finding the Heart's True Home. California: Harper.

Fromm, Erich. (1956). The Art of Loving. New York: Harper & Row.

Green, Michael. (1975). I Believe in the Holy Spirit. Michigan: Wm. B. Eerdmans Publishing Company.

Hammond, Frank & Ida. (1973). Pigs In The Parlor. Missouri: Impact Books.

Hart, S.L. (1968). Lifetime of Love. Mass: Daughters of St. Paul.

Johnson, Spencer, MD. (1998). Who Moved My Cheese? USA: Penguin Group.

Lancaster, Wade & Jeanette. (1982). "Rational Decision Making: Managing Uncertainty". Journal of Nursing Administration. Sept. 1982. pgs. 23-28.

Leman, Dr. Kevin. (1981). Sex Begins in the Kitchen. California: Regal Books.

MacNutt, Francis, O.P. (1974). Healing. Indiana: Ave Maria Press.

Martin, Dr. Walter. (1962). Essential Christianity. California: GL Publications.

Martin, Francis P. (1979). Hung by the Tongue. Louisiana: F.P.M. Publications.

Maxwell, John C. (2023). The 16 Undeniable Laws of Communication. Maxwell Leadership Publishing

McAll, Dr. Kenneth. (1982). Healing the Family Tree. Great Britain: Sheldon Press.

Moody, Dwight L. (1881). Secret Power. California: Regal Books.

Murphy, Dr. Ed. (1992). The Handbook for Spiritual Warfare. Tennessee: Thomas Nelson Publishers, Inc.

Nutrition Search, Inc. (1973). Nutrition Almanac. New York: McGraw-Hill Book Company.

Payne, Leanne. (1991). Restoring the Christian Soul Through Healing Prayer. Illinois: Crossway Books.

Peck, M. Scott, MD. (1978). The Road Less Traveled. New York: Simon & Schuster, Inc.

Peck, M. Scott, MD. (1983). People of the Lie. New York: Simon & Schuster, Inc.

Penner, Clifford & Joyce. (1981). The Gift of Sex. Texas: Word, Inc.

Powell, John. (1969). Why Am I Afraid to Tell You Who I Am?. Illinois: Argus Communications.

Powell, John. (1974). The Secret of Staying in Love. Texas: Argus Communications.

Powell, John. (1976). Fully Human, Fully Alive. Illinois: Argus Communications.

Powell, John. (1978). Unconditional Love. Texas: Argus Communications.

Ross, Elisabeth Kübler-. (1960). On Death & Dying. Simon & Schuster/Touchstone.

Sanders, J. Oswald. (1967). Spiritual Leadership. Illinois: Moody Bible Institute.

Schaeffer, Francis A. (1971). True Spirituality. Illinois: Tyndale House Publishers.

Seamands, David A. (1981). Healing for Damaged Emotions. Illinois: SP Publications, Inc.

Smalley, Gary & Trent, John, Ph.D. (1986). The Blessing. Tennessee: Thomas Nelson, Inc.

Smalley, Gary & Trent, John, Ph.D. (1988). The Language of Love. California: Focus on the Family.

Smalley, Gary & Trent, John, Ph.D. (1990). The Two Sides of Love. Colorado: Focus on the Family.

Smith, Chuck. (1980). Effective Prayer Life. California: The Word for Today.

Swindoll, Charles R. (1983). Dropping Your Guard. New York: Bantam Books.

Taylor, Richard Shelley. (1962). The Disciplined Life. Minnesota: Bethany House Publishers.

Holmes TH, Rahe RH. The Social Readjustment Rating Scale. J Psychosom Res. 1967 Aug;11(2):213-8. doi: 10.1016/0022-3999(67)90010-4. PMID: 6059863.

Torrey, R.A. (1974 revised edition). The Person & Work of the Holy Spirit. Michigan: Zondervan Publishing House.

Vine, W. E. (1981). Vine's Expository Dictionary of Old and New Testament Words. New Jersey: Fleming H. Revell Company.

Watson, David. (1980). The Hidden Battle. Illinois: Harold Shaw Publishers.

White, Tom. (1993). Breaking Strongholds: How Spiritual Warfare Sets Captives Free. Michigan: Servant Publications.

Whitfield, Charles L., M.D. (1987). Healing the Child Within. Florida: Health Communications, Inc.

Wilkerson, David & Sherrill, John & Elizabeth. (1963). The Cross and The Switchblade. New Jersey: Spire Books.

Wilkerson, David. (1972). The Pocket Promise Book. California: Regal Books.

Williams, Dr. Roger J. (1971). Nutrition Against Disease. New York: Pitman Publishing Corporation.

ABOUT THE AUTHOR

My heart's cry is one of freedom and abundance for you, who read this. I was born and raised in the Panama Canal Zone and accepted Jesus Christ as my Lord and Savior between the ages of 10-13. During my childhood, God called me off by myself to spend time with Him reading His Word, next to the sparkling blue Caribbean water. He was my teacher and even with that, many mistakes did I make! When I was 17, He called me to be a Registered Nurse and it was during one of my areas of work that an earlier edition of this book was born.

I married at 22 to an unbeliever, was divorced at 30 and went through what I call baptism by fire during my first marriage. God had me clean up all I was doing that was unloving nor supporting my marriage regardless of what my ex-husband was or was not doing. Doing what is right because it is right, is the right thing to do though it's not easy. Especially when my own needs were not being met! The earlier edition of this book was completed during this season of life, and I began teaching these kingdom principles of living a victorious life in the community for many years.

During the writing process, there were times that I stopped as I did not know what the next step was. I sought the Lord, and He answered me through a sense of knowing. Only then did I move on and continue writing. One summer, I remember sitting at my desk while the sun was shining brightly on the deep-colored greenery outside my window. I looked at everyone playing while I sat working with the sun playing on the leaves. I chose to not get up and play because, above all else, my heart's cry is one of freedom and abundance for you who read this. Even then, I knew that to create something requires sacrifice and I knew that I would either get my reward later or maybe never. And the reward didn't even matter. What was and still is important, is that I finish the work I promised God I would and was called to do.

I have since remarried, have a wonderful family and look forward to more of God's blessings in my life as I give to others! May you ask Him for your way and follow it. Therein is fulfillment and blessings galore. Why else are we to be here but to live out what was ordained for each of us from the beginning of time? That is why this work was written. That is why this work was written for you.

With blessings always,
Nancy Williams

www.ingramcontent.com/pod-product-compliance
Lightning Source LLC
Chambersburg PA
CBHW060816050426
42449CB00008B/1681